Mr.
Baitenswitch

Ghost Stories
to Keep You and Your Organization
Alive

Mr. Baitenswitch
Ghost Stories
to Keep You and Your Organization
Alive

Underground Wisdom Version

©2019 J. Thomas Sparough

All Rights Reserved

Space Painter's Publications
4228 Delaney Street
Cincinnati, OH 45223
513-542-1231
SpacePainter.com/books

ISBN 9780977290253

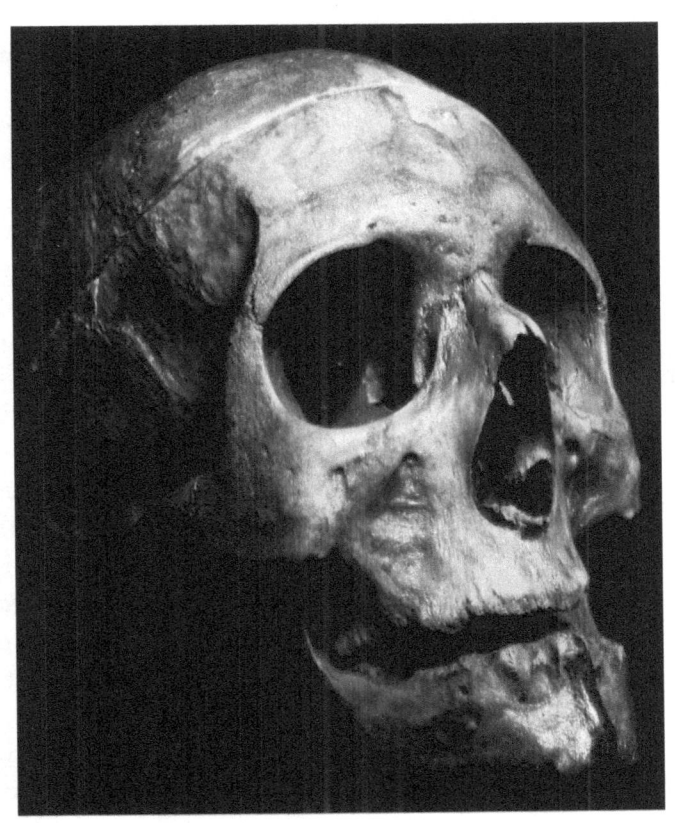

Acknowledgement

I gratefully acknowledge all the people who helped me to craft these ghost stories. I wrote the collection in a single month. Most days, after I finished a story, I headed over to Michael and Joan Hoxsey's condo, where our family and friends were gathering. One of us read the newest story. I will forever treasure those family conversations in the last months before Michael's passing.

Thank you to Patrick Donnelly for encouraging me to write the stories. The subsequent editing of the project was a three-year process and involved dozens of people. Thank you to all who offered their musings, questions, corrections, and encouragements.

Special gratitude goes to my fellow Storytelling in Organizations board members, including Pete Griffin, Trisha Griffin-Carty, Cora Newcomb, Stuart Rothgiesser, Julienne Ryan, and Mark Steiman.

And I would especially like to thank those people who read the entire collection and shared their feedback with me. They include Sarah Asebrook, Joe Conrad, Lyn Ford, Kateri and Travis Gries, Tricia and Peter Hupperich, David Hutchens, Joseph Sparough, J. Michael Sparough, and my partner Geralyn Sparough. Without all of you, this collection would still be haunting me.

A final thanks goes out to my brother, W. Stephen Sparough, who helped me to finish this project, and who long ago sat next to me in bed as our mother read kid-friendly scary stories to us each night.

JTS

Contents

Forewarning

Today, storytelling illuminates the organizational world. Corporations, non-profits, and government have gathered around the fire of story, but in limited camps. Until now, the campfires of organizational storytelling have not included ghost stories. Mr. Baitenswitch changes that.

This collection of fictional ghost stories is spine-tingling wisdom. It is intended to be a captivating way to stimulate thought about important topics in organizational work. There are a great variety of stories in it—spooky, humorous, touching. The stories are about embracing the positive and finding the path to be fully alive, both individually and organizationally.

This technique is a form of generative storytelling. Although some are cautionary tales, each story is intended to help generate reflection on these life-giving topics. In a reference section in the back of the book, there are two sets of questions for each story. The first set is focused exclusively on the story. The second set is a chance to explore the topic personally. After the questions, there are a few thoughts offered by the author.

One use of this book, in addition to thought-provoking entertainment, is an alternative to business case studies. In the back of this book, there are indexes for themes and settings. These may be useful to managers, trainers, and facilitators looking for an appropriate story to share concerning a specific need.

It is my hope that through this book, a match will be lit in the darkness that can engulf each of us. And in that match light, we will ignite our own stories. Those stories are like a campfire, which brings clarity, warmth, hope, safety, and excitement to our lives and careers.

J. Thomas Sparough

Dead-icated
to my friends and colleagues
of the Storytelling in Organizations
Special Interest Group
of the National Storytelling Network.
Because of your inspiration, this book is
alive.

Deadline

The words echoed in Tricia's mind, "If you are late with another project this month, even one minute late, you will be fired."

Tricia was working furiously, orchestrating the keys of
her computer. It was 10 minutes before 11 p.m. She would not
be late, not this time.

She felt her analysis was strong. It had information in
it that others would not have noticed. She told herself that was
why she was still in her cubicle long after everyone else had gone
home.

Yet, she was not alone.

Brent had entered the office without a sound. Since he
had been fired, he was not allowed in the building, but he liked
to come in late at night and lurk. No door could stop him. Once

in the office, he would open up desk drawers of people he knew, searching to find something that would amuse him, some sign that they were having trouble keeping up with their work, like a cautionary memo from the boss.

Tricia continued to type. It was now seven minutes before 11, which was the absolute deadline of her property analysis report. She was on her final paragraph. She had done the research for this report, made phone calls, looked up old records. She had gone above and beyond. There, the report was finished. Now all she had to do was proofread it.

Brent noticed that there was a light on in the big room, the room that housed 48 cubicles. He went toward that light and came to Tricia's workstation. Now he was staring at Tricia's back as she crouched over her screen. He silently rubbed his hands together and smiled.

It was three minutes to 11. Tricia was going to get this report filed on time. At her performance review last week, her boss said that she was chronically late and apparently couldn't be relied upon to turn in anything by a fixed deadline.

She had objected to this comment. Her boss had told her, "The proof is in the pudding. Don't be late again on any project this month." And then those echoing words, "If you are late with another project this month, even one minute late, you will be fired."

She found a typo and corrected it. This report would be just on time.

Tricia didn't see Brent. She didn't know that he was there. Really, he was only half there, but he understood what she was doing. She was certainly trying to finish a property analysis by the standard 11 p.m. deadline.

Two minutes left and only one more page to read. Tricia was on schedule.

After he had been fired for repeatedly missing deadlines, Brent had gone to the bridge and sat there for what seemed like hours. He was mulling over all the ways that other people were as incompetent as him. Why was he the one to get fired? He decided to show everybody that he had a spine, that he had courage to follow through, that he could finish something.

He slid off the bridge and hit the water with his back first. Death did not come instantly as he had hoped. He drowned slowly, tasting the river as he swallowed and gasped. At the moment of final departure, he emerged out of his body and floated to the top of the water. When he climbed onto the shore, and made his way into the city, he could not dry himself. Brent felt continually wet and cold.

He wanted revenge. He wanted others to suffer his unjust fate.

He went down to the floor and slithered towards Tricia. He was under her chair, and she had no idea. He reached out and touched one of her legs.

Tricia jerked her knee when she felt the touch. It was a sudden cold spot on her calf. She kept her focus, though. She was finishing reading the last page. She had one final minute to file her report.

Brent turned his attention away from Tricia's legs. He put his hand on the computer power cord and pulled.

The screen went black. Tricia hit the space bar a couple of times. "No, what, no."

Tricia shook the screen. She pushed her hands across the keyboard hitting random keys. "What's going on? This isn't happening. No, no, no." Tricia stood up for a second. The large digital clock on the wall said "11:00." She looked at her computer. She saw the cord was out of the wall socket.

"Oh, crap." She plugged it back in.

She turned her computer back on. Three seconds later it chimed as it started to reboot. The screen flickered and slowly began to glow. She pressed her hands against her face as she watched the screen come to life at a snail's pace.

Her document did not come back up.

It was now 11:01. She located the report on the desktop. She sent it without looking to see if her changes had been saved. In the morning, she would explain what happened. The clock said 11:02. Tricia picked up her purse, grabbed her coat, and walked out of her cubicle.

At that instant, a chill went through her, as though she had just stepped outside on a cold day. She shivered and at the same time noticed her hands suddenly felt moist. She wiped them on her dress. What could have made her hands wet? Tricia had the feeling that someone was looking at her. She looked around the office. As she did, she was overcome with the reality that she would be fired. Whatever people said about her boss, she knew he always kept his promises.

Tricia felt a cold spot on her calf once again, another shiver. She quickly walked out of the room and came to the elevator. She pushed the down button. While waiting, Tricia thought, it hadn't been her fault. The plug was loose. It was unfair. She should be rewarded for her extra work, not fired.

Brent was still at the entrance of Tricia's cubicle. When Tricia had walked through him, he fell to one knee, laughed, and clapped his hands together. He smiled from ear to ear. Since Tricia was just standing there, he grabbed at her leg before she walked away.

Now, Brent heard the elevator door open. He waved goodbye with both hands. Tricia had made his night. Perhaps later he would meet her at the bridge.

Probation

People said that the spirit of Frank L. McColumn lived on at the McColumn Pump Company. Strange things happened there, and people attributed them to Frank. Those strange things were usually good things, but not for people on probation.

Whether or not his spirit was actually in that 97-year-old building was debatable, but the fact that Frank's picture was everywhere in that building was undeniable.

At the McColumn Pump Company, one of the 100 best companies to work for in America, every new hire had a 90-day probationary period. When Marv Green was hired, he soon learned that a surprising number of people didn't make it through the 90 days.

The old man's son, Franky McColumn explained, "It's

13

not that we fire them. They quit on their own accord, but those who make it through the 90 days usually stay with us for their entire career."

On day 27 of Marv's probation, Marv was signing an invoice when his pen went dry. He shook the pen and then carefully put it back on the paper to continue his signature. But it still wouldn't write.

Marv grabbed another pen off his desk and tried to finish his signature. It wouldn't write either. He shook it and tried it on some scratch paper. The paper ripped, but there was no blue mark from the pen. He opened a desk drawer and grabbed another pen. It didn't work either.

Leaning back in his chair, Marv took a breath. His eyes locked on the framed photo on the wall. Frank L. McColumn was staring at him. Marv closed his eyes for a second and breathed in through his nose. He had seven pencils, but not a single pen that worked.

The weird part, thought Marv, was that he had used all those pens recently. How could they all stop working at once?

"Carmen," Marv said to the woman at the next desk, "would you happen to have a pen I could borrow?"

"Sure," she said. Marv took it and tried to finish his signature, but this pen wasn't working either. "This is so stupid," uttered Marv under his breath. "I can't even write my damn signature."

"Sorry, Carmen. Your pen isn't working," he said as he handed it back to her.

A sudden pain in Marv's stomach made him grimace. His mind entertained the thought that someone had tampered with his pens. Perhaps it was a plot to make him look bad, or stupid?

He got up and walked across the room. The eyes of Frank L. McColumn were on him. It gave him the creeps.

"Mr. Montez, would you happen to have a pen I could borrow, one that works?"

"For you Marv, of course."

"Could you make sure it works?"

Mr. Montez paused, looked carefully at Marv, and then smiled. He drew one straight line on a piece of paper and handed the pen to Marv.

Marv went back to his desk, signed the invoice, and then got up and returned the pen. He nodded to the picture as he passed it. He stopped and looked more carefully. Shining in the picture was the slim metal clip of a pen in his front shirt pocket.

Back at his seat, Marv picked up his pen from his desk. He tried it on the scratch paper, and it worked perfectly.

On day 52 of his probationary period, Marv printed out a six-page budget report that he was going to share at the staff meeting. He had 11 copies of the report. He paged through the top copy.

"Shit, the pages are wrong," he said out loud. He looked at the next copy. The last page was on the second page. The fifth page was on the sixth page. The copier had always collated the pages correctly. What was going on?

He briefly thought about reprinting it, cringed at the thought, and decided it was too late anyway. He sat the 11 copies on the floor. He could see that people were already going into the meeting room. The photo of Mr. Frank L. McColumn was staring right at him. He was leaning against a copy machine with his elbow on the glass and his chin in his hand.

Marv pulled out the staples one by one. He rearranged the first set and stapled it together. He double-checked the page order. It was correct. On the fourth set, as he was shuffling the papers, one of the pieces of paper sliced into his index finger. Paper cut. "Damn." He sucked his index finger. How could a piece of paper cause such pain?

Chuckling to himself, Marv thought, "He works through the pain. This Marv is really something!"

A moment later, Marv arrived at the meeting room with his stack of 11 perfectly collated budget reports. He noticed the boardroom had a photo of Frank L. McColumn passing out papers to people at this very table.

It was day number 80 and Marv had been invited to lunch with several people. Marv came out of the bathroom, his hands thoroughly washed and dried, and headed to the elevator where his group had already formed.

"Hey Marv," said one of his coworkers. "Have a little trouble in there?"

Marv laughed nervously. "No trouble. I am an expert, you know."

"Well, Mr. Expert, you got a little something on your shoe."

Marv looked down to see a piece of paper towel stuck to the bottom of his shoe. "Oh, jeeze, ahh, just a minute." He awkwardly walked back into the bathroom. Leaning up against the wall he pulled off the paper towel.

There was a piece of gum stuck to the sole of his shoe. He took off the shoe, grabbed the pencil from behind his ear, and dug out the gum. It was soft and came out in a stretchy mess, smelling of cinnamon. He cleaned his pencil with a paper towel, and then decided to just toss the pencil out. He got his shoe back on and washed his hands. There was a picture of Frank L. McColumn next to the mirror. In the photo, he was holding a red pack of gum.

As Marv started to walk out of the bathroom, he felt something sticky under his foot. It was the other shoe this time, another piece of gum, stinking of cinnamon. A bead of sweat appeared on his forehead. He started to lose his composure but then calmed himself. "This is nothing," he said out loud. He fished his pencil out of the trash, cleaned his shoe, washed his hands, and joined the others for lunch.

Day 89 was a Friday, and Marv pulled into the office lot at 6 a.m. He was trying to finish up a demonstration chapter of the instructions for the new accounting software. This project wasn't expected until late next week, but his plan was to have it finished by the 9 a.m. meeting. He wanted to leave a good impression on his last day of probation.

Marv swiped his key through the slider at the front-door entrance. A red light flashed. Above the light was a bronze plaque of Frank L. McColumn. It had an inscription that read: "Through these doors walk the best workers in the world."

Marv thought, "Yeah, if they could just get in the door." He swiped his key again, another red light. The staff was scheduled to start arriving at 8 a.m., but he had been told the door was open to him 24-7. He tried swiping the key very quickly, then slowly, and then what he thought was normal speed. Nothing worked.

Back in his car, he pulled out his computer. He would just work in the car. He looked at the street lamp in front of him. Of course, there was a poster of Frank L. McColumn on it, and he was staring into the car. Marv sighed and opened his document. The low battery notice popped up on his screen. "You're kidding. I charged this thing last night."

Marv plugged the laptop into the charger and put his car key in the ignition. He turned the key. There was a clicking noise. He pulled the key out, reinserted it, and turned the key. The car wouldn't even turn over. "That's just great," he muttered. He stared at the poster. He wondered, "What would Frank L. McColumn do?"

There was a diner across the street that caught Marv's eye. I'll go work in the diner. And so he did.

At 8:03 his report was finished, and he tried his car. This time it started right up. "Figures," he said. His key worked at the front door, too. At 8:45 he clicked on the print icon. He strolled over to the group workstation. The printer came to life, and its rollers began to turn.

His paper did not come out, though. The yellow light began to flash. "How much bad luck can one guy have? It's jammed." He walked to the back of the printer and turned it off. He glanced at the picture hanging above the work desk. Marv said to the picture, "What's up with you and printers and copy machines?"

Marv opened the back of the printer and pulled out the jammed piece of paper. He shut the printer door, turned it on, and hit the OK button. The printer came back to life, cycled through, and then went quiet. Marv blew out a big breath, marched to his desk, and hit print. Then he went back to the printer. Nothing was happening.

"Carmen, the printer isn't working. Can you give me a hand?"

"Sorry, we are not supposed to fix it. Alan has to do all the repairs."

Marv noticed he was clenching his jaw. He thought, "Five minutes until the meeting starts, and I don't have the chapter that I worked my ass off to get done early."

He said, "Is there anything we can do?"

"Just wait. Alan will be here this afternoon."

Marv walked down the hall and opened up the door to the stairwell. He needed a moment by himself. Inside the stairwell, he slowly and gently banged his head against the wall.

After a minute, he walked back to the door, turned the knob, and pushed. He couldn't open the door. It was jammed shut. The back of the door had a picture of Frank L. McColumn. The almost life-sized photo was screwed into the metal door. Frank was pictured with his arms crossed standing in front of the door.

Marv pushed again, but the door wouldn't open. He banged on it a couple of times. No one came.

He walked down a set of stairs and tried to open that door. It wouldn't open. He went down to the first floor. That door was locked tight. "This is a fire trap," he thought.

"Claustrophobia," he said out loud. There were sweat marks under his arms.

There was one window in the stairwell on the second floor. He walked up to it. He looked out at the parking lot below. He felt an urge to get out of that stairwell, to jump through the window.

He put both hands over his eyes. He pounded his palms onto his head. He wiped his face with his fingers. He knew what he needed to do.

Marv walked up the steps to the door with Frank's picture. He pounded on the door. No one came. But he didn't stop. He kept pounding. For two minutes, he pounded on the door. No one came. Three minutes and 28 seconds later, Carmen opened the door.

"There you are! The meeting has started. We were all wondering where you were."

"I have been trapped in here. The doors won't open. This stairwell is a fire trap!"

Carmen looked at him. "Are you OK?"

"I think so. I guess I had a panic attack when I couldn't get out."

"Marv," Carmen said, "I think I know what happened. Stay in there for a second and see if the door will open now." She closed the door. Marv was now staring at Frank's picture once again, but his arms were no longer crossed. He was smiling and had his arms outstretched. Marv's jaw dropped, and then he smiled back at Frank L. McColumn. Marv turned the knob and opened the door.

"Come on to the meeting." The way Carmen said "meeting" sounded to Marv like something special was about to happen.

As the two walked into the meeting room, there was applause. Franky McColumn said, "Marv, congratulations. Since 90 days ends on Saturday, we have decided to make it official today. Your probation is over. We welcome you to our staff." More applause.

"The old man tests everybody. You've come through with flying colors," Franky said. Now there was laughter. Marv looked around the room, lots of smiling faces. There in the meeting room was another portrait of the old man, Mr. Frank L. McColumn. He was smiling, and he seemed to be looking right at Marv.

Carmen said, "Marv, you've made it, and I think you're going to find that the man who started this company is going to become your new best friend. Once you have won him over, things are never the same."

20   SPAROUGH

Ghosting

Sitting at the hotel bar by himself, Gene noticed Lee Ann working on her computer at a nearby table.

"Can I buy you a beer?"

She answered, "No, but I'll take a scotch and soda." She had nursed her way through a rum and Coke, giving her the energy she needed to finish her monthly expense submission.

It turned out to be a blessing in disguise that Gene's wedding ring was at the jewelers for repair. He told her he was recently divorced. She told him she had never been married because she was always too busy at work.

Gene thought that Lee Ann had the most joyful laugh.

One drink later, they went their separate ways. In the morning, though, they saw each other at breakfast and exchanged emails and phone numbers.

Gene, of course, only gave her his office information.

They met three other times before they became lovers.

A couple months after that, Gene received an email from Lee Ann that she had been diagnosed with breast cancer. She wrote, "You are the rock to keep me stable. You are the person who brings me joy and hope."

It was too much for Gene. He thought it prudent not to respond to the note. So he ghosted her.

There were other emails, a series of texts, and five voice-mail messages. Gene did not answer any of them. Then the relationship died, or at least one member of it, painfully quick over the course of 13 months. Gene had no idea of the torment Lee Ann suffered through, how his disappearance plagued her right up until the day of her lonely death.

Just after the passing, Gene was stamping a few letters using the office machine. Although there was a rule against using this machine for personal mail, Gene was careful to mix his business mail in with his birthday card to his sister.

As he stamped the envelope to his sister, Lee Ann came into the room. She was wearing a soft white dress, and her long black hair was out of control, just the way Gene liked it.

She caught Gene's eyes, raised her own eyebrows, and strutted out of the office.

Gene normally loved this kind of attention, and he was excited, because she looked good, but coworkers might have seen what just happened. "She shouldn't have come to my office," he thought, "even if she is feeling better."

Yet he hoped he would see her again soon.

The next week Gene was doing something that he did about once a month. He was taking a hooker to dinner. This month her name was Polly.

For Gene, the best part was that he had devised a way to expense the dinner. She was a potential client. The dinner would be reimbursed by his company. And the hooker gave him 50% of her services.

Polly had gone outside to smoke a cigarette when Lee Ann walked over to the table and sat down in Polly's seat.

Lee Ann put her finger to her lips and then pointed at him. "Don't say a word. Just listen. I want you to know that I have been watching you. Following you. I've got my eye on you, but don't worry, I'll be business discreet."

With that, she got up and seductively strolled out of the restaurant.

Gene wanted to get up and follow her, but he had a business arrangement with Polly. There was money involved. "Business before pleasure," he said to himself. He had his way with Polly in the back of his car and went home to his wife.

The next day, Gene was in the restroom at the office. He did a little trick that he enjoyed, which was to urinate a tiny bit on the floor in front of the urinal that he knew his boss always used. It gave him a chuckle.

Laughter rose up in that marbled bathroom from one of the stalls. It was Lee Ann's laugh, sheer delight. Gene had that sound embedded in his head after their nights together.

He zipped up and turned toward the stalls. There was the laughter again, muffled this time.

His mind buzzed. Afternoon delight. In the men's room. While he was on the clock. This was a good day. Crazy. But good.

Gene opened one of the stall doors. No one was there. He let it swing shut. The squeak of the door echoed in the bathroom. He opened another door. No one was in any of the stalls. Gene was alone and walked out of the washroom disappointed and confused.

The next week, he was coming back from the office at 11:30 at night. He was exhausted, but had a sense of accomplishment. Once again, he would be the top salesman of the company.

He had gotten into the sales program on his boss' computer. Once in, he used his statistical method of adjusting the sales numbers by never more than a half percent. He knew the report summary used whole numbers and rounded up and down.

He took .2 from Bob, and .4 from Lashonda, .4 from

Larry, and so on and so forth, and added them to his numbers. His fellow sales staff never had their whole numbers changed, but they lost a percentage here and there, and all that they lost was his gain.

This self-made sales winner had just turned on to Ravine Street when he heard a little rustling in the back of his car. A hand came out of nowhere and touched his shoulder.

Gene screamed and swerved the car on to the shoulder of the road.

Lee Ann laughed. She managed to pull herself between the seats to get into the passenger seat. "Did you miss me?"

Gene steered back onto the road. He said, "Oh my God, you are crazy. You nearly scared me half to death."

She said, "Sorry, but I really did want to see you again!"

Lee Ann moved toward him and kissed his neck.

"Should I pull over?"

"No, there is no time for that. I want you to know that I did love you, but I am here to tell you goodbye. You have come to the end of the road and look where it's gotten you."

The car missed the turn and went through the edge of the guardrail and plunged into the ravine, crashing through the forest, and abruptly stopping at a 90-year-old oak tree.

After the crash, there was the sound of steam exiting the cracked radiator. Lee Ann effortlessly exited through the shattered windshield, but then leaned back into the car. "Sweetie, now you will be able to see everything clearly, but I am afraid I won't be able to see you anymore."

Gene had a tree branch stuck through his chest. He could hear Lee Ann speaking. She looked like an angel. He started to say something, his mouth moved, but he had no breath.

His life began to flash before his eyes. Slowly, despair took hold of his heart.

Dead Serious

Sue fastened the Velcro cuff to take the blood pressure of her young patient, Elroy. She pumped up the bladder and began to check the pressure, slowly letting out the air. It made a hissing noise that somehow today seemed louder than usual.

The pressure was low, as expected, but acceptable. Sue pulled the sections of Velcro apart to take off the cuff. That hissing noise was stuck in her head, "Sssssss sssss."

Perhaps this was one of the consequences of working a double shift, and not only from this double, but the two others she had pulled this month. "Sssss." She looked up at the ceiling. Was something leaking? These hospital rooms were full of air and gas lines.

Standing still, she listened. She heard the beeping of

monitors and sounds out in the hallway, but nothing like that hissing noise.

She turned toward Elroy and adjusted his pillow, got him a cup of water, and brought him a blanket. He was cold, and she knew his prognosis was poor. She wasn't sure she could take another death so soon.

As she stood looking at Elroy, predicting his future, the noise came back. It was changing, though. It seemed to be someone saying her name. "Ssssuuue. Suuuue."

Sue looked at Elroy quizzically. "Did you hear that?"

"Hear what?"

"Someone was saying very quietly, 'Sssssuuue.'"

"No, I didn't hear anything."

"Well, it was probably nothing." Sue walked out of the room slowly, as if expecting to hear the sound again. She knew she was exhausted. She shook her head back and forth very quickly to wake herself up.

Sue had the best of intentions when she got into nursing and specialized in oncology. She truly wanted to make a difference, to help people in their time of need, especially children and their families.

Lately, it had been quite taxing on her. Sue took the job very seriously. She knew her work was a matter of life and death. Administering the wrong medication, or the wrong dosage, could cause death.

Even with the right medicines and the best care, people died. Tara O'Conner had died last week from leukemia. Tara was always making up jokes. Sue remembered as she was trying to get her to eat, Tara asked, "Who's the relative that likes to sleep on your lap at dinner?"

"Napkin!"

Even on that very last morning. Tara had asked, "What animal loves to run around naked?"

Tara didn't give Sue a chance to answer. "The bear!" Tara started to laugh at her own joke, and then cough, and then she couldn't breath. She died shortly afterwards.

Sue had felt responsible. She knew that was irrational, but she still felt it. She didn't have the right words to calm Tara down, to keep her breathing. And there were others, lots of others in her career. Lashonda, Bret, Margaret, Jin, Allison, Winter, and Patrick were in the last four years. In that hallway, working on her computer, she felt like she didn't know how to do her job anymore.

An hour later, as she was entering more patient data, the voice returned with the click of her keyboard. "SSSSuue. Ssss ssss Suuuue suuuuuicide."

Sue swallowed hard. She looked around. She tapped her ear with the palm of her hand. She had thought about suicide before, but not recently, not since her ugly divorce, and losing two beautiful patients in the same month.

A veteran nurse of nearly 20 years, she needed to focus. It was her job, she reminded herself, to pay attention to every detail. She couldn't be thinking about one thing, while doing another.

As Sue spent time in her three rooms, talking to each of her patients, trying to make them comfortable, there was a little buzz, like a mosquito that wouldn't leave her alone, and the noise it made was "Sssssssssssssuicide."

She heard it when she turned on the faucet to draw water. She heard it when Elroy sipped on his straw. She heard it as the door swung shut.

Back in the hallway, she thought about Tara's death. Tara didn't seem to care about instructions. She didn't seem to take anything seriously. Sue had never been able to get through to her, to get her to sit still, to get her to be quiet, to get her to just read a book.

Tara had asked, "Why do monkeys like bananas more than books?"

"Bananas are more appealing!"

At home that night, Sue fell asleep quickly, but awoke about 2 a.m. She went to the toilet and then got back into bed. In the dim glow of the city lights coming through her bedroom shades, she put her night mask on, closed her eyes, and lay upon her back. A moment later, she turned to her side. A couples minutes later, she turned to her other side.

Her mind was whirling. She felt her life was a train wreck. She never talked to her irresponsible sister. She had divorced her irresponsible husband. Her track record with cancer patients felt pathetic. She began to cry. She pulled up her eye mask. The message from earlier in the day came back in her memory, "Ssssuicide."

The next morning at work, she was dispensing a cup of coffee in the break room, when the voice started up again as the coffee steamed and hissed into her cup. "Suuue sssuuuicide."

With both hands, she wiped her brow and cheeks. She puckered her lips. She felt like she couldn't breath. She managed to walk out of the room.

As she stepped into the hallway she smelled the disinfectant. A thought surfaced. Although the hospital tried hard to make the aroma of their cleaning products pleasant, if ingested in a large enough quantity, they would kill a human.

She managed to force that thought out of her mind and take a long breath. She had serious work to do. Sue made her rounds and wrote her name on the white board in each room.

Later that day, she felt exhausted. Once again, she was taking Elroy's blood pressure. The hissing of the air coming out was transposed into one word being repeated, over, and over again.

"Sssssuuuicide. Suicide. Suicide."

Sue finished and slowly walked out of the room. Mindlessly she found herself opening the door to the stairwell and walking up one flight of stairs after another. She made it to the roof and opened the gray metal door. She walked onto the patio of the roof. The door swung shut.

In a kind of trance, she moved toward the ledge. She could easily climb over the solid glass fence that separated her from an 11-story fall. The roof air conditioning unit was whirring and creating a kind of hissing noise. All Sue could hear was

"Ssssssuuiciide."

She covered her ears. Her emotion overcame her. It was her fault. All of it. Every mistake. With her family. Her husband. Tara. All of them.

Taking hold of the glass wall, she lifted herself over it. She stood on the ledge looking below to the emergency room entrance. There was a driver by an ambulance smoking a cigarette.

Sue let out a sob. She felt she was ready to listen to the voice that plagued her thoughts.

Standing on the ledge, leaning toward the ground, Sue looked across the parking lot and saw a tree. She thought it would be good to have her final resting place be under the shade of a tree.

With a slight breeze suddenly blowing on Sue, she heard a new voice. "Do you know why cats are afraid of trees?"

Sue stood still. What was she hearing?

"Because of the bark!"

This friendly, young voice said, "Look how blue the sky is."

Without questioning what she heard, Sue moved her gaze from below to above. The sky was a beautiful, deep blue with some puffy, white clouds moving across it.

Emotion overcame her again, and she snorted in agony, putting both her hands around her nose and mouth. She took three rapid breaths.

She clearly heard, "You're a good person."

Sue said out loud, "I am not a good person." She thought she was talking to herself.

She braced herself to jump. The voice continued, "I always knew you cared about me."

Suddenly, Sue's mind went blank. Her eyes closed. She listened, "That is why you were so strict, because you cared."

Sue held her breath for a second and opened her eyes wide. She grasped the patio fence. She recognized that voice. Could it really be Tara?

Sue took a deep breath and listened. The wind was blowing. She could hear the leaves of the tree fluttering in the wind. The hissing noise was gone. She could still hear the air conditioner, but not the hissing. Wiping her cheek, she was quiet for about 90 seconds. She was looking at the ambulance, the tree, the cars, the people walking. She climbed back over the glass barrier onto the patio.

Sue walked over to a set of chairs and sat down. Looking up at the sky, she felt strangely calm and knew what she wanted to do. She was going to take a break from nursing. She was going to talk to her sister. All this flashed through her mind as she watched the clouds. They kept changing shapes, which reminded her that she could change, too.

After some time, she stood up and walked across the patio. She turned to look at the tree, which made her laugh out loud. Then she opened the gray door and walked down the stairs.

Down the Stairs

Cool Concepts was an ad agency that had moved into its new office about a month ago. They had a six-month lease with an option to buy.

The place was great, except for the rats, or whatever they were. That is why the Cool Concepts owner had not purchased the property. She wanted to see how things went for the first six months.

On the first Friday of every month, the entire staff went out to lunch together. This time, though, Melinda wasn't feeling well, and so she stayed at the office as everyone else left. When the last person went through the front door, the place was suddenly silent. Melinda realized it was the first time she was alone in the building.

It was a 140-year-old storefront in amazingly good condition, perhaps because it had been vacant most of its existence. None of the staff had actually seen a rat. But there were two unoccupied apartments above the storefront.

Two weeks ago, a guy moved into one of them. He didn't even make it through one night. Something had attacked him, and his face and arms had ragged cuts in them. Melinda had heard him say, "I swear it wasn't a rat."

One of Melinda's coworkers had said that she was told that the previous tenant had brought a shaman into the building to rid it of an evil spirit that dwelled there. The shaman had said the ghost-like creature was ancient and lived in the soil below the building. It was angry that people had built upon its land.

No one really believed that story, but now that Melinda was in the building by herself, she felt a tingle of discomfort.

She went into the kitchen. It was February and dreary. She turned on the little space heater. She wished she had worn pants today. Her legs were cold.

Melinda turned on the electric kettle. Suddenly, the space heater, the lights, and the kettle all went dead. "Damn," she thought, "the circuit must be blown." She knew exactly where the circuit breaker was located. It was in the creepy basement.

There was a trapdoor in the hallway, which led to the basement. Melinda pulled the ancient metal handle and propped the door up next to the wall.

She peered into the darkness below. The light switch for the basement was located on the pillar at the bottom stair. Melinda pulled free the flashlight that was held on the bottom of the basement door. She turned it on. A strong beam emanated from its glass lens.

She stepped down onto the first step. She counted the steps…10, 11, 12, 13. She thought to herself, "Who makes a staircase with 13 stairs?"

Melinda did not think she was brave. In fact, she was so nervous that sometimes even answering a phone call was difficult for her. Opening her own closet door late at night could give her the shivers. Yet, she was pragmatic. She needed the kitchen to have electricity. She pressed through her fear and walked down the steps.

As she reached the 6th step, a spider web caught Melinda's face. She cringed and quickly wiped it off her face and hair, trying to free herself from the sticky threads. She continued down the basement steps.

With high hopes, she flicked the switch for the light. Nothing happened. Instant disappointment. She wondered, "How many things can be on the same circuit?"

Melinda shined the flashlight around the basement. The walls were made of stacked limestone filled with cracks that were perfect for spiders and anything that needed a nest in a dark room. The floor was made of stone as well, but because of the flooding over the years, the sediment that lay on top of the stone made it a dirt floor. It was littered with nails, yellow newspapers, a coil of wire, and four small bundles of what appeared to be sage or some other herb.

She walked quickly across the basement to get to the door of the room with the electric panel. Her feet made a squishing sound with each step.

As she put her hand on the clammy doorknob, she was overcome by the smell of the basement. It brought her back to the yard at her parents' home. There was a stump in the backyard that had this smell. The smell was of things rotting underground.

She wondered what was rotting in this basement. At her childhood home, Melinda remembered walking past the rotting stump holding her nose. That smell made her sick to her stomach. She complained about it to her parents and her grandmother. Then one day, she and Granny dug all around the stump. They wore bandanas over their nose. Granny hooked a chain to the stump and pulled it out of the ground with the truck. They found a dead animal wedged under the roots. They hauled it to the dump. After that, the smell was gone.

Now in the dark basement, her stomach was sick from the putrid smell as she opened the door. It was a stone room, a chamber really. Shining the light on the electric panel, she stepped towards it. The smell caused her to put one of her hands over her nose. With a slight creek, the door behind her shut. She stepped back to it and pushed it open. Again, the door creaked shut. Melinda ignored it and went back to the panel.

The door of the circuit breaker was already open. With the beam of the flashlight, she searched the little glass bubbles until she saw the one that had turned red. She placed her hand on the black lever and pulled it down and then up.

At just that instant, her flashlight fell from her hand. She was suddenly engulfed in darkness.

She bent down and put her hand on the slimy ground, hoping that she would touch the flashlight. She didn't feel the flashlight and began to move her hand about the mushy, cold floor searching for it. Her stomach churned from the rotting smell of the room and the discomfort of touching the floor.

She felt something brush by her face. She screamed. That sound of terror was amplified in the small stone room, which startled her, so she screamed again.

"Stay calm, stay calm. Find the flashlight."

She felt something touching her legs. She screamed again and fell onto her backside.

A stinging pain on top of her hand, then another on her forearm. She was being attacked. She let out a series of sobs and backed herself across the floor into a corner. She felt spider webs, and then a spider crawl across her cheek. She put her hands over her face. The backs of her hands were being bitten. She shook them around her head, but she couldn't feel what was biting her. Whatever it was, it didn't seem to have a body.

This was clearly not a rat.

As she cowered in the corner, something flashed through her mind, a sign she had seen in Colorado, what to do if attacked by a wild animal—fight back.

Melinda let out a scream, a mixture of fear and adrenaline. She began to punch and kick the air.

Then she thought, "I have nails, too." She bared her nails

and began to slice her fingers through the room.

She felt her stomach being scratched. Melinda yelled, "Leave me alone." She began to spit into the air. She slashed her nails through the darkness. Whatever was attacking her seemed to suddenly back off.

Melinda began to slide against the uneven stone wall toward the door. She pushed through the cobwebs, moving her hands and feet, keeping her back against the wall. She came to the door. It swung open and she fell through.

She righted herself and ran towards the stairwell. She flipped the light switch on, and the basement was ablaze with florescent light. She heard a low howl, like an animal in pain.

Melinda felt sick as she saw her bloody arms and legs. She was covered in the slime of the floor. Spider webs were on her clothes.

Up the steps, one, two, three, four, five, six, seven.

On her ankle, a tug and a bite. She kept going.

Eight, nine, ten.

It pulled her back. She fell onto her knees.

Nine, eight, seven. She was being dragged back into the basement, her stomach against the steps.

She flipped herself over so that she was sitting on the step. She screamed, "Let go!" She kicked, punched in the air, and started back up the steps.

Eight, nine, ten, eleven, twelve.

Pain swept over her. One more intense bite on her leg.

She kicked like a mule and rose up out of the basement. She slammed the trap door shut.

She raced to the front door and stumbled outside. There was blood all over her body. As she stood shivering in the cold, one thought kept going through her mind:

"We will dig that thing out of the ground and be done with it forever."

The Founder

Dear Reader,

Now I see that I was wrong, but I can't change the past. I remember that I spoke to Michael in his dreams. "Are you going to let my company fall apart? Get off your lazy butt and get back to work."

Two weeks after my funeral, my beloved Michael went back to work. "Better late than never," I thought. It hadn't occurred to me that he was actually mourning my death, that he loved me despite our differences.

I am ashamed to say that what did occur to me was that the upstart moved into the boss' room. My room! Mr. Hugh North, the founder of the company. That is ridiculous, of course.

But, honestly, I was outraged.

Michael left my desk and chair in the office, but he removed my antique lamp, my original rotary phone, and my floor-to-ceiling filing system.

As he sat in my leather chair, I spoke to him as if he could hear me. "You have no right to move anything. Follow my orders."

Michael slowly pushed his hands over his ears like he was a child. He cleared his throat and mumbled, "Leave me alone." The veil between the living and the dead is thin.

For 47 years, I ran The Constant Call Telemarketing Firm. For 23 of those years, we were the largest telemarketing company in the nation. My son joined the business in year 31, just as we had started our decline in market share. Michael was fresh out of business school and full of new ideas to bring us back to our former glory.

He was telling me what to do! Gradually, he got my message. "I don't take orders from anyone. The rules of our firm were set years ago, and those rules have led to our success. Change the rules over my dead body."

After my death, I thought my spirit would become the voice of reason in his head. But, he was headstrong and wouldn't listen. Within a week of taking charge, he gathered a group of nine employees into my workroom.

I named them The Inept Nine.

"As you know, I am not my father. I believe that each of you has an important role to play in helping to decide the future of Constant Call. I want to work together to ensure the growth of our company."

I had never been afforded the chance to go to college and resented those who thought they were better than me because of it. My hard work and clear leadership built my company. My son didn't seem to understand that.

I said to Michael, "Fool, you know nothing. People need the iron fist of management to feel secure in their duties! If you give people choices to do anything, they will flounder. They need clear direction!"

For years, I had been fighting the winds of change that were a constant threat to a solid organization. I had a proven system, and it was stupidity to mess with it. Sure you tweak it, but you don't change it. Over time, I was sure my market share would return.

My son and his team decided "to expand modalities and embrace new systems. Current times required current methods."

"No," I shouted into his ear. "If you lose the core methods of my business, your energies will be scattered and wasted."

Shortly after that, he had my desk and chair moved into the basement. Then, with the complete backing of The Inept Nine, he put the building up for sale.

As the memo to the full staff read, "We are streamlining our operations, ensuring job security, and moving into a state-of-the-art facility."

My heart sank. That building represented my greatest accomplishments in life. I felt something stirring inside me. It wasn't anger. It was remorse. I asked myself, "Why is he doing this?" Imagine that, a dead man pondering the questions of life.

It took me weeks to honestly answer that question. I didn't want to face the truth, but it came into focus. I saw that I hadn't listened to my son since he had been back from college. I longed for the days of his youth when he did everything I asked of him without question. My pride came tumbling down. I sank into despair as I saw that I was the one who needed to change.

Yet, I still didn't want to lose the building. On the day the important papers were signed, the contract went into the old-fashioned mailbox on the edge of my parking lot. What were they thinking? Had they not heard of registered mail?

There, as twilight descended, I put my hand and arm into that mailbox and pulled the letter forth. A strong rain was falling, and I dropped the letter into the gutter and watched it wash down the grated drain.

About a week later, my beloved son Michael came to my building late at night, 11:37 p.m. to be exact. I was in the basement, sitting in my chair thinking about the cancer that had eaten my body.

"I know you are here," he shouted. "I am tired of you trying to run my life. I don't know how you did it, but only you could have stopped that deal."

I heard the elevator engage. A moment later the door opened, and he was in the basement. It was good to see him, even if he was angry. He got a dolly and managed to get my desk onto it and into the elevator. Over the next two hours, he removed all of my things and wheeled them into the side parking lot. On the final trip, I rode with him in the elevator. I looked into his eyes wishing he could see me, and hear me clearly. I said, "I'm sorry."

He dropped his head and ran his hands through his hair. "I'm sorry, too," he said under his breath. I could see that his eyes were moist from the disappointment of this task. The elevator doors opened. He wheeled the last cabinet to the parking lot.

It was all there in a pile: my lamp, my chair, my filing cabinets, even my favorite coffee mug. He got a five-gallon can of kerosene out of the trunk of his car. He poured it on my things. It streamed out of the can and splashed all over my possessions.

My mouth was open in disbelief. I whispered in his ear, "Don't do it, son. It's yours now. Save it."

He shook his head as if he heard every word and whispered, "You are dead. It is my company now. How am I supposed to move forward with you trying to control my life?"

My son left the empty kerosene can on my desk.

Pulling out a pack of matches, he struck a match against the flint. The yellow flame flashed in the darkness of the parking lot. He tossed it onto my leather chair. Engulfed in flames, I watched my chair, my desk, my lamp, my life burn to the ground.

My relationship to my son went up in flames. When the blaze was over, Michael said in a choked voice, "Time to move on. I'm done with you, Dad. I can't let you hold me back anymore. I have a business to run. I have to figure out how to pay the bills. And my family needs me more than you do." He got into his car and drove off.

He left me crying in the smoldering parking lot. So now, months later, I am sitting in the corner of the basement in my empty building. I am lonelier one day to the next. I know it is time for a change, but I don't know where to go.

I will put this note in a bottle and drop it down the same drain I used for the contract. If you are reading this, please help me. Perhaps you have found both the bottle and the contract? Would you be so kind as to deliver them to my son? I don't know how to move on without him.

Sincerely,
Hugh North

Mr. Baitenswitch

In his cubicle at the call center, he tried to picture himself in his safe space. It was the beach at Siesta Key, Florida. "Hello, this is Brendan of customer service. May I ask your name?"

"My name is George Baitenswitch."

"Well, good afternoon, Mr. Baitenswitch. How may I assist you?" As Brendan said these words, he wondered if this man was a heavy smoker. How else do you get a gravelly voice like that?

"Call me George."

"Absolutely, George, how may I help you?"

"My life is over, and I am very unhappy."

Brendan thought this was a joke. Lots of callers had an odd sense of humor. He smiled. "George, my friend, you called the right guy. I specialize in making people happy. I am going to do everything I can to resolve your issue. Now what seems to be the trouble?"

"The problem is I've got no life left. I am forever in the dark."

"Let me put it this way, George, what product are you calling about today?"

"I am calling to get a new life. You are my lifeline."

"George, I appreciate your call and wish you all the best, but I am afraid you have called the wrong number. This is Amazing Products customer service. I can only help you with product information."

"Your product is the reason that I am miserable, why I am stuck in the dark."

"Mr. Baitenswitch, which product are you referring to?"

"Do you want the product ID number or its name?"

"Either is fine."

"Then I'll give you both, you little weasel."

"Either is fine, and there is no need for name-calling. I am here to help you."

"You have already told me you can't help me, that you care nothing about me."

"Please, just give me the product information." Brendan took a deep breath and tried to imagine himself on the beach at Siesta Key. The warm sand on his feet was a soothing feeling. He needed to stay calm.

"One, seven, three, alpha, seven, bravo, two. The Ever Light."

"Thank you. I'm pulling that up. I see the item is discontinued, but maybe I can still help. What seems to be the issue with your Ever Light flashlight?"

"It doesn't work."

"Say a bit more about that. What exactly is the problem?"

"The problem is I am talking to an idiot who doesn't care about me or my flashlight."

Brendan tried to see the gentle waves at the shore of Siesta

Key and feel the salt water on his bare feet. "Mr. Baitenswitch, I really am trying to help. Did you drop the flashlight?"

"How would I do that?"

"Perhaps you bumped into some furniture, and it slipped out of your hand?"

"There is no furniture here so it couldn't have slipped out of my hand. You have a lifetime guarantee, don't you?"

"We do have a lifetime guarantee. When did you purchase it?"

"It was given to me as a present seven years ago."

"Well, George, we have a new line of flashlights, and I can provide you with a replacement."

"No, I want this one to work, because I am stuck in here. All I have is a phone and a flashlight, and the flashlight doesn't work, and it's your fault, you piece of scum. Did you get that message, Brendan?"

"Loud and clear, sir. And I thank you for your call. I truly hope things improve for you."

Brendan disconnected the line, pulled off his headset, and stood up. It felt like he had some sunburn from his day at the beach. He walked to the break room. He opened the refrigerator and stared inside. The cool air felt good. His cheeks were flushed. He grabbed an apple.

"How's it going?"

Brendan looked at Rachel and took a bite of the apple. He shook his head. "I just talked to a certifiable nut job."

"He got to you?"

"A little, and I have to say I hate this job, at least with calls like that one. Truthfully, I am not so sure that picturing my safe space is helping."

"Do you think a different place might help?"

"I don't know," Brendan said.

"Maybe a mountain view would help. You often talk about your hike on the Continental Divide in Colorado. Maybe that's the place where no one can disturb your calm."

"I guess. I do love the mountains."

"Give it a try, and let your supervisor know if you get too stressed. Anger will take you away if it gets hold of you."

"Really, Rachel? Do the mountains help you to stay so calm?"

"No, I pretend I am on a trampoline, and everything bounces off me."

Back at his desk, Brendan put on his headset. A call came in. "Hello, this is Brendan of customer service. May I ask your name?"

Silence.

"Hello, this is Brendan of customer service. May I ask your name?"

Silence.

"Hello, are you there? I can't seem to hear you. Can you hear me?" Brendan disconnected the call.

Another call came in. "Hello, this is Brendan of customer service. May I ask your name?"

Silence.

"Can you hear me?"

Silence…no wait, soft, raspy breathing. Brendan listened carefully. He could clearly hear breathing. "Hello, are you there? This is customer service."

No response. Brendan disconnected the call. He tried picturing himself on top of the Continental Divide. He breathed in the crisp mountain air. He hit speed dial one. "Hey Bob, I have had a couple of calls in a row that I couldn't hear anyone. I wanted to make sure that there isn't a problem on my end. Can you give me a test call?"

A call came in. "Brendan, can you hear me?"

"Yeah, Bob. Thanks."

"Thank you, Brendan. I appreciate you following our protocol."

Another call came in. "Hello, this is Brendan of customer service. May I ask your name?"

Silence.

"Hello?"

Brendan heard a wheezing breath. A voice he recognized said, "Hellll-o."

It was the gravelly voice of Mr. Baitenswitch. Brendan thought about disconnecting immediately but stayed on the line. He was at the Continental Divide and looking at the pine trees below. But with 17 call reps, how the hell did he get this guy twice?

"Brendan, I need something from you."

"What's that sir?"

"I told you to call me George. I'm your friend."

"Yes, of course you are. George, how can I help?" Brendan tried to feel the mountain breeze and see the clear blue sky.

"I want you to step into my shoes for a minute."

"Go on. How would that help?"

"Because you are a whiny little punk who has no idea what I am going through."

Brendan snapped the pencil he had been holding in his hand. "I am going to have to end this call."

"Don't you dare end this call. I am stuck in this coffin with nothing but a phone and a flashlight, and the flashlight doesn't work. I need you to fix this."

Brendan was speechless. He hit disconnect. He tapped his chest with the palm of his hand to slow down his heart. He closed his eyes and tried to get back to the Continental Divide.

Another call. He hesitated to connect. Brendan tried to imagine a mountain meadow of flowers. He laughed to himself, and connected. "Hello, this is Brendan of customer service. May I ask your name?"

"You know my name. Come see things from my side. Come experience eternal darkness while you have the Ever Light in your hand, the hand that has never dropped the light."

"Sir, I don't know how you are calling me, but I am going to have to ask you to stop this. It is not funny. I can't help you. Have a good day." He disconnected. He was out of breath. Perhaps the altitude was too high. He needed to get back to the beach.

Ten seconds later, a call came in. Brendan looked at the light that signaled the call. He didn't answer. He imagined himself jumping on a trampoline at the beach.

That low, gravelly voice came into his earphone anyway. "You've got no spine. You don't help people. You manipulate them. You abuse them. You leave them hopeless and in the dark."

Brendan fell off the trampoline. "Get off this fricking line." Brendan was in a rage. "I am not listening to you. You're a pathetic sicko. You deserve to be dead. I wish I could see you, see you in all your pain, you cigarette-smoking idiot!" Brendan was smashing his fist against his desk.

As he was screaming, he lost touch with where he was. It felt as if he was being sucked away from the call center into the phone line. He was somehow in the phone line, darkness, speed, anger, whipping along. He left the trampoline, left the beach, left the mountains, left his cubicle, and was compelled into darkness.

Rachel and a half dozen other people stood up and stared at Brendan. He appeared to be in convulsions. Then he calmed down suddenly. He opened his hand and looked at it. He took off his headphones. He was smiling. He took a long slow breath.

Rachel shook her head at him. "I guess someone is getting assertive. Brendan you really lost it. Management is going to be all over that exchange. I thought you were going to break your desk the way you were hitting it."

"You know," he said in a gravelly voice. "Call me George."

In the sudden darkness, Brendan could not see anything. He opened and closed his eyes. There was no difference. He lifted his arms. They hit against some kind of padded roof. He was stuck lying down. In one hand was something that felt like a phone. In the other was a cylinder, a metal tube with a switch. He pushed the switch forward. Nothing happened.

Bottom Line

In the graveyard, the place where my wife and my parents were buried, I lay wide-awake in my casket. I felt completely alone in the darkness. Something unpleasant was growing inside of me. At only six feet underground, it seemed the weight of the world rested on my soul.

As the CEO of Furniture of the Future, I worked my whole career for a healthy bottom line, and although I was successful, I had regrets. Now they were growing.

After my death, for two days I left my body and walked the streets near the funeral home. Nothing interested me. So I went back into my body and waited for my final rest.

A week later, I felt empty and sleep deprived. For some reason, I was being drawn out of my grave and back to my company. I needed to get up and do something. It may sound funny to you, but it was utterly depressing to me.

My bodily spirit emerged from under the fresh sod of my grave. I was fully dressed in my burial suit, but I was only there in spirit. I could see through my hands, through my clothes, my legs, and even through my shoes. I began to walk away from my grave towards the industrial side of town. It was a 9-mile trip to my company. I had never walked that far in my good shoes.

My feet dragged but did not kick up dust as I walked. It was an effort to move, but mindlessly, I walked to the place I had worked for 42 years, 26 of them as the CEO.

It occurred to me that I had always heard that no one dies and wishes he had spent more time working. Yet, I wasn't headed to see my daughter, or my son, or my grandchildren. My family had always been my first priority. I guess that beautiful life was complete. I was headed back to work for unfinished business.

As I arrived, I was surprised to find there were lots of people like me, dead retirees that had been drawn back to work.

"Hello, Peter." It was the voice of Steve Nelson, one of the deceased engineers.

"Hello, Steve."

Dozens of people had come back to work after they died. I found them everywhere. They all had a regret that wouldn't let them sleep. They were restless souls, and they were hiding. I met Sasha up in a tree looking out at the company campus. I found Harold in a janitor's closet. Demarcus and I met on top of the factory roof.

They were ashamed of their predicament. That is why they hid. I easily located them. Every time I got near one of them, I had a tingling sensation where my heart once beat.

I found Juan under the table in one of the product development buildings. He had been the North Star of the marketing department.

"You won't believe why I am here," he said.

"Try me."

"Years ago, I had an idea that came to me in the shower.

It was a design for a new chair that we could offer. I told my manager about it, but he told me to stop joking around and to do my job. I never got the chance to do anything with my idea. My job was to sell other people's ideas."

I looked closely at Juan. He was biting his lip and pressing his hands together as he hid under a table. He looked like a defeated man. He was stuck in pain. How could that be? He had been one of the most successful members of our company.

I had to help him. "Do you still want to share your design?" I asked.

"It's too late," he said.

"Better too late than never," I said.

Sitting under the table together, we looked across the room at the design team. They looked young and alive. "Let's wait until they finish work today," I said.

When the room was quiet, Juan took a pencil in hand. It's hard to do that when you're dead, but if you want to hold or move something badly enough, you can force your energy to it. He willed the pencil to move. He sketched out his design on a piece of paper and left it on the desk of one of the designers.

The next day, that designer picked up the sketch and studied it. She began to smile. She asked if anyone knew where it had come from. No one knew, but everyone loved it. "Awesome, and I love that it has five legs," one of the team members said.

They built prototypes of that chair. After work, Juan and I sat in them and talked about old times. I told him something I had never told any of my employees. "Secretly, I have longed to be a poet. I always wanted to send out a memo that was a poem rather than a company announcement about another new policy."

"You should do it," he said.

Perhaps this story is the start of my poem. I am sharing my heart with you.

When the chair went into focus-group trials, on the second day, the response was so positive that Juan just started floating away. His spirit was soaring. "Thank you, boss," he said to me as I stretched to give him a high five.

Something powerful came over me as I watched him relax and float out of the building. That moment helped me to recapture a bit of my heart from the regrets that had sprouted in it.

I came across Judy in a storage closet sitting in her old chair. "Judy," I said, "what are you doing here?"

"Hi, Peter. Well, you know, same old same old."

She had been a standout project manager. My heart ached for her as I heard her say, "I never did what I truly wanted to do."

"What was that?"

"I wanted to stop the infighting. I wanted to create an atmosphere of empathy and understanding in our office."

In her 35 years with the company, she oversaw 11 multi-year projects. Her teams were known for getting along with each other.

"Judy, you were one of our best team leaders. Your people worked exceptionally well together. What more could you have done?"

She looked at me and didn't say anything. I could tell she was struggling to speak. Tears of light welled up in her ghostly eyes. Finally she said to me, "Were you blind?"

"What do you mean?"

"I mean," she said, "did you not see the way the male workers harassed the women workers. Did you not hear the disparaging comments about our African American employees? Were you not aware that one of your gay workers took his own life after a practical joke played on him in the factory bathroom?"

"I, I don't know what to say. I tried to create a positive work environment."

Judy said, "I know you did. And I am not mad at you. I am disappointed in myself. It is all I can think about. My life is over, and I am consumed with regret. I had wanted to do something for years while I still was alive, but a busy project manager like me couldn't jump ship for a year or two to concentrate on collegial-relationship building." Judy shook her head. "So why do I feel like I missed my calling?"

Standing silently with Judy in the storage closet, my own eyes filled with tears. Such sadness surrounds death. She looked at the floor. Her tears were like jewels of light hitting the ceramic tile by her feet. I wiped my cheeks. My tears were warm like sunlight. "Maybe it's not too late," I said.

Over the next few days, we created and left guides about critical conversations so that the right people would notice them on their desks. We sent out emails with short poignant stories. We put up a photo of Sid Burns on the entrance wall, the man who had taken his life after the restroom incident. The plaque under it said, "In loving memory of Sid, a loyal worker who we all miss."

On a Tuesday evening, Judy said to me, "It will never be enough to change everyone, but it is enough to comfort me. My regret is gone."

Watching Judy in the darkness of the afterhours, I saw her rise up out of her chair. She began to laugh softly. It was time for her to take her final rest.

She said, "I'll never forget you." She floated out of the room.

How can I say this? Since my death, I have felt incomplete, like I had missed what was truly important at work. I had let my employees down.

Now, what I wanted most was to help others succeed with their unfinished business. My time with Judy and Juan helped to ease that burden. I set out to replicate that success.

I helped Demarcus join the phone sales staff for a day of phantom calls. Sasha got to use the woodworking tools and actually made a coffee table. Harold got involved in resource management and saved the company more than $10,000. Steve got to hire a square dance caller for the monthly employee luncheon. He danced every dance, even though he couldn't hold on to a partner.

Time flies. In the last year, I helped 89 retirees let go of regret. Eighty-nine, that's how old I am. I am sitting in the chair of the current CEO. Her grandfather clock will strike midnight soon. Then I will turn 90 years old.

Sitting in this chair, it occurs to me that by keeping people in one job, they get put in a box. We slide the boxes around strategically and call it job freedom, but the people are still in the box, stuck in one role with unfulfilled dreams.

Take it from me. You are going to end up in a box once you are dead. It's not right to put people in a box while they are still alive.

I mentioned that I always wanted to share some poetry, but it never seemed to fit my role as CEO. It seemed too soft. Perhaps helping people is poetic? Poetry goes beyond the mere meaning of the words. What I experienced over the last year cannot be fully expressed in a written statement. What can one say to the living about the struggles of death? Your time will come soon enough, and then you will know for yourself.

I decided to take Juan's advice to share a poem. This poem is for our current CEO. Maybe someone alive can still make sense of it? Maybe she will feel the impact of what these words mean to me. I am leaving it on her desk.

The Bottom Line

Unfulfilled dreams don't die
Regret sprouts in the lonely darkness
Cultivate dreams today
Cross-pollinate the business garden
Grow the future while the light still shines

My hand trembles. I leave the poem on her desk. A dream I have had for 20 years, I have fulfilled in 20 minutes of clutching a pen with my death grip.

I notice that I am smiling. My heart is full. The clock is chiming. I'm turning 90.

I feel light, like the chimes of the clock resounding in the room. I am floating off the floor, out of the room, through the building. It is effortless. Now, I soar off the company property, down the back roads. I don't need to walk. I am floating through the air, watching the night sky. I see the distant planets burning steady.

Now, I float over the iron gate of the cemetery and come to my grave. The grass has just been cut. The moon is but a sliver. My spirit descends through the grass and dirt to my wonderful, comfortable casket, my final resting place. My dream is about to begin. My eyelids grow heavy. My heart is content. I close my eyes, and my final sleep comes at last.

Working Dead

Mercedes Jefferson was a master interviewer. She was known to pick just the right person for just the right job.

Not this time.

She bit her lip as she remembered her interview with Brian Tombwater. He had the right qualifications, yet her gut said, "No."

She had felt her stomach tighten when he said that retirement was not fulfilling, that "work was all that mattered."

Mercedes ignored that gut feeling, or more accurately, rationalized it away. She needed someone with his skills. His idiosyncrasies would be tucked back in accounting.

When she hired him and shook his hand, it was limp and dry. "Lifeless" was the word that came to mind. She glanced at her hand after that handshake. There were flakes of his skin on her palm.

Six months had passed. Today, she called Tombwater to her office for his progress review. She didn't typically give these reviews, but Tombwater's direct supervisor, and his workstation lead, had recently resigned.

She waved her hand motioning for Brian to come into the office.

"Brian, hi, have a seat."

He came in. She recognized that gait, that slow, steady walk, like he hadn't a care in the world. She smiled at him. It was a forced smile. He looked like hell and smelled like a compost pile.

"Well, thanks for coming in."

He spoke in a drawn out, low voice, "You're welcome."

"As you know, your immediate supervisor, Peggy Kwon, very recently resigned from her position. So, today, we are going to have your six-month review."

"Thank you. I have been looking forward to hearing how I am doing."

"Let's get started then."

"Yes, let's get started." He repeated her words but had taken all emotion out of them.

"Your work, Brian, is excellent. You seem to have immediately mastered our input coding. Everything you have done has been efficient and accurate."

"I work hard to make it so."

"Yes, you do work hard. You are known to be one of the first ones in the office and one of the last ones to leave at night."

"I live for my job. It keeps me alive."

"Brian," Mercedes brought her lips together and searched for the right words, the path to expose the unpleasantness in the room. "Are you happy?"

"Yes, I am very happy."

"I mean, are you happy outside of your work?"

"I have already told you that my life is my work. Without

work, what else is there?"

"Brian, your personal life is none of my business, but I have always believed that a healthy personal life is just as important as a healthy work life. Do you find that to be true?"

"I find that I AM my work. It is what keeps me going."

"You have certainly made quite an impression around here. Your handwritten notes have beautiful penmanship, and they are direct in their messages."

"I know that I am the only one who handwrites notes, but I do that as a backup system, in case the electronics fail."

"Brian, we have a triple backup system so I don't think you need to handwrite your notes as a precaution."

"But, what if all the electronics died? Death can come in an instant. Then what would we have as backup?"

"That is not a question for you or I to answer. Let's get back to your review."

"Is there more?"

"Yes, there is. Your appearance, Brian, is important. The way you look matters. We give our employees great latitude in this area, but it is clear that you need to make some changes."

"I haven't really noticed."

"You never comb your hair. For a while people thought it was just your style, but it has become clear that you not only don't comb it, you never wash it. And you are wearing the same suit that you were wearing on the day I hired you."

"I like to look good. I wear my suit."

"Your suit has not been dry cleaned in ages. It has tears in it and stains all over it."

"I hadn't noticed. It is not important."

Her gut said, "Fire this man immediately." But there were reasons she needed him.

"Yes, Brian, the way your suit looks, the way your hair looks, and the way your shoes look are all important. In our handbook, there is a written expectation that every employee will display an appropriate, professional appearance."

"But, it is not a specific rule."

"Brian, it is common sense, and I am about to say something else that is very important. Your job depends on it."

"I am listening."

"Brian, you smell. There is an odor coming from you right now that is making me very uncomfortable. If you don't change this behavior, you are going to be fired. Here is an action plan for you. After this interview, you are going to leave my office and the building. Go home, clean yourself up, change your clothes, and comb your hair. Then you may return to work. Is that clear?"

"Yes."

"Do you have any questions for me?" she asked.

"I do have a question for you. Are you happy with your work?"

"No, Brian. I meant do you have any questions about what we have just discussed."

"I would like to alter the action plan." Brian's eyes widened. He opened his mouth like he was yawning.

She could see that his teeth were decayed.

He pushed backward in his chair and took a long deep breath in. Then he leaned forward, his mouth still wide open.

Mercedes heard it before she saw it. The sound was like wind rushing through a tunnel. Brian's eyes were fixed on her. She couldn't break away from his gaze. To her horror, she saw an orange and slightly purple stream of his breath coming towards her.

Her hair fluttered and the collar of her dress rustled as the stream of his foul stench reached her. She pursed her lips, but it went upwards through her nostrils and coated her eyes. The sound and the smell seeped into her ears and penetrated her brain. The toxic cloud covered her insides. She felt it burning her, surrounding her, smothering her.

Her head flopped backwards and her mouth opened wide. The putrid stream of orange and purple intensified, shooting down her throat. Her eyes began to roll and drool covered her chin.

He released his gaze and closed his mouth. He relaxed in his chair.

She slumped over her desk, groaning. After about 30 seconds, slowly she sat up as her eyes cleared. She took out a piece of paper and set it on her desk and began to write without hesitation. She signed her letter and left it on her desk. Mercedes reached into her drawer and got her purse, stood up, and walked out of the office.

He said to her as she left, "Good day."

Brian Tombwater got up from his chair, walked around the desk, and sat down in Mercedes Jefferson's chair. He glanced at her resignation letter.

His action plan was beginning. It was time to hire people who lived for their work.

Cold Hearted

When I heard Julie say that it was no surprise what had happened to me, I decided to teach her a lesson. Nobody deserves to die from road rage.

It is true that I was a hothead, but I've cooled off. Death will do that to you.

The average worker is no different than me, Julie included, and I decided to become a teacher to point this important lesson out. My new job is to help people to get along better so they don't suffer my fate.

There is a learning curve, though, and I enjoy imparting my lessons. I admit that I've become a mischievous teacher, but I give daily lessons to the company employees.

Since Julie and the others often witnessed me get worked

up over nothing in the company break room, I picked the perfect little cubicle right there as my teaching environment. I like my cool, dark space. Can you guess where I picked?

Most days, everyone comes to me because they need something stored in my office. It feels good to be needed. One by one, they come to my little classroom. Each time they open the door, the light comes on.

I may be nothing more than a ghost, but the president of our company comes to me and bows down as she uses my services. And everyone follows her lead.

People come and open my door and stand and peer into my cubicle. I hold them spellbound. They try to decide what they want, why they have come to me. Several days this summer, I think it was for the cool air that poured out when my door was open.

Awhile back, I got the idea to simply change the place where people left their supplies. I put the old things where the new ones were laid.

It was a worthwhile teaching moment. All I did was exchange some things that had been on my shelves for six months with the things that were brought in that very day.

One by one, the people shouted, "What's this! Who has been messing with my stuff?" They looked right at me, but they couldn't see me. The teachers of life's lessons are often hidden.

The day I was killed, someone had tailgated me as I drove home from work. There was no room for me to speed up, but that car raced into the other lane, passed me, and then cut back into my lane in front of me. Then they slowed down. I got so angry that I smashed into their bumper. Eventually, we pulled over to the shoulder. It was there he shot me three times.

Here in my office, another teaching technique I developed was to keep my door open during the night. Therefore, everything warmed up to the office-wide temperature, including my heart. I do love my pupils. Many of the items on my shelves were sensitive to this warming. The blower in my office tried to keep everything cool, but it couldn't.

The next day, the teaching continued. "The cream has gone bad overnight," they screeched. "This soda is warm!" they said in disgust. It ruined their whole morning. They sent in a repairman who couldn't find anything wrong.

I took his assessment as a vote of approval. My job is to keep the difficulties coming until they learn the lesson.

Little Miss Perfect, Julie, still has a lot to learn about relaxing and keeping things in perspective. She is one of the people with the biggest reactions to my concealed efforts. A mere fingerprint in her materials got her to bite her lip to the point of bleeding. She stormed off with fire in her eyes. How is that different than road rage?

I often think about the day of my death. Why did I get so upset about a disgruntled driver? The whole incident might have taken me one extra minute to get home. Instead, it cost me my life.

Julie and the other employees thought they were getting organized by putting nametags on their cans, bottles, and packages. I laughed as they carefully placed their supplies on my office shelves. Once they closed the door, I went straight to work. I pulled the nametags off and switched them from one item to another.

My students had no idea they were being tested. When they found their nametags were on the wrong items, they accused each other of foul play. Julie whined, "Stay out of my stuff, or you'll be sorry!"

Sometimes, I am half in my cubicle and half out. I can't leave my workspace, but I can stretch myself. Every good teacher does. This way, I get to see every reaction to my lessons.

Doug, who had only been with the company three weeks, saw his nametag was on the wrong package. His eyes bulged, and he threw his stuff across the room, splattering spaghetti sauce all over the wall, and he refused to clean it up. He quit right there in the break room.

It gives new meaning to "break room."

One day, I got hold of a marker, and I changed the name

of Joe to Julie. It was sloppy but effective. My students are on edge over the littlest of things. Joe started screaming at Julie. He was upset to the point that he threw his back out. He fell over in pain.

Really, people need to get a grip. It is time to learn the lesson: Little things shouldn't make you crazy. I lost my life because I never took that lesson to heart.

As a teacher, I don't mind the mess, the spills, and the stale items that no one will claim or discard. I like the company of the unclaimed yogurt cup on my back shelf.

One of the strongest learning opportunities I gave was to open up their drinks and take a sip. Then I put the caps back on crooked.

Fireworks, I tell you. Fireworks in the office when people saw a bottle with a cap that had been opened. Julie got so upset it sent her straight to the bathroom! No surprise there.

Today, I unwrapped the tinfoil on Julie's package and took one big bite. Then I put it all back together perfectly. She'll soon discover her next lesson. Perhaps she'll show improvement?

I am feeding all the employees important information. If my students could hear me talk, I would say to them, "Learn my lesson about what really matters, or die trying."

I am going to keep doing what I do. I am stuck in the cold, but I don't mind. Teaching warms my heart, even if my office keeps it cold.

Stone Faced

Joseph wasn't a night watchman. He worked the day shift, but tonight he was filling in, which he did infrequently and reluctantly.

In the dead of night, Joseph left his co-worker and walked into the dark of the art museum to do the rounds.

The sound of his footsteps echoed as he walked through the entrance lobby, past the ticket counter and information desk, towards the main stairwell.

He made his way to the upstairs gallery. The motion sensor switched on the lights, although only to half power. Everything was dim and shadowy.

He came to the Native American Arts room. It was filled with pottery, masks, and weavings. Joseph himself was filled with resentment and defiance, upset with having to cover this shift.

In the center of the room, there was a life-sized bison and a bear. These were roped off to keep the visitors from trying to touch them. The bear was standing on its hind legs and towering 9 feet into the air.

The bison was positioned standing in grass but looking to the side, like it had just spotted a threat. Joseph examined it for a moment and then did what no visitor was allowed to do. He stepped over the rope and stood next to the bison. "Why shouldn't I get to do something nobody else gets to do?" he thought. "I'm stuck here in the middle of the night. I can do whatever I damn well please. It's the least the museum can do for me as I give up another good night's sleep."

Joseph ran his hand over the side of the bison. It felt warm, like the animal was actually alive. Joseph put his ear next to the nostril of the bull. It sounded like the bison was breathing. He laughed at that thought. He positioned himself nose to nose with the bison and whispered, "Whatcha got big fella?" There was a snort that seemed to come from the bull. That startled Joseph. He took a couple of steps back right into the bear.

Joseph let out a short scream as he realized he had backed into the bear, its fur touching his neck. He lost his balance and slipped to his side, which caused him to fall on the exhibit rope. One of its stands tumbled over, making a loud clank as it hit the tile. Joseph stayed on the floor for a few seconds, his heart pounding. As he set the stand back in place, he said to himself, "I really don't like this. It sucks. I hate walking through here at night."

He continued his rounds, walking down the service steps and into the storage and work area, a room as big as a football field with art that was crated, sheeted, or boxed.

There were also worktables, where the art was cleaned and repaired. On one of these huge tables was a sheet cloaking an item about 6 inches tall. Joseph was curious. It felt like he deserved to see what was under that sheet. After all, Joseph wouldn't see his own sheets tonight. He lifted the white fabric to see a small statue of a smiling man carved out of stone.

He picked up the statue and examined it. He guessed he was holding something that was more than two thousand years old. Joseph looked at the ancient face. It stared back at him, but it had no eyes, just indentations where the eyes should have been. Joseph continued to look at the face of the statue and soon found himself in a trance-like state. He couldn't break his gaze as he looked into the eye sockets of the statue.

He thought, "Put it down." But he couldn't. His vision began to blur. In his imagination, he saw his own eyes set into the statue's face. Joseph felt a pressure in his cheeks and forehead. His face was inching toward the statue. He could hear his blood pulsing through his head.

Forcing his eyes shut, he separated his gaze from the little statue. When he opened his eyes, he was careful not to look directly at it as he set the statue back on the table. Joseph thrust the sheet over the statue and walked out of the room.

He was out of breath as he climbed the stairs back to the main floor. He was almost done with his walk.

Joseph took a deep breath as he entered his favorite part of the museum. He tried to relax as he walked among the life-sized statues from the Renaissance era. He could feel his heart pounding. It was a mix of excitement and fear. Joseph decided he was going to do something else he had never done before. He would touch one of the statues, but he became worried that someone was watching him, not from the cameras, but from here in the room. He couldn't shake the feeling that he wasn't alone. Joseph didn't think that there were other people here, but he wondered about the artwork itself. Did it have life?

He paused and looked at one of the masterpieces standing before him. It was a combination of two figures. One was of a man, powerfully built but damaged. His head was missing, and his left hand was gone.

Joseph knew this was a valuable piece of art, carved out of marble by one of Michelangelo's students. Even without the head, it was a stunning piece.

The woman, who was the other figure in the duet, was staring at the man, smiling, leaning, and reaching for him. She was barely dressed with a cloth covering her. Her hair hung down below her shoulders, her head tilted.

Looking at her stirred something deep in Joseph. He felt a sense of melancholy. She was forever reaching for her lover, who had lost his head.

How did that happen? Was it damaged in the making so that he never had a head? Or did vandals some hundreds of years ago knock his head off?

Joseph decided to follow through with his desire. He reached out and touched the lady's arm. It was cold and not exactly smooth. He thought that it would have been perfectly smooth, but it had a roughness to it.

He looked closely at her eyes. They were carved out of stone, not nearly as convincing as the glass bison eyes. Yet, there was something about them that was entrancing.

Joseph saw a dark spot under one of her eyes. He looked closely, and it appeared to be a tiny bead of water. Perhaps a leak from the ceiling had caused it. That was a comforting thought to him, for Joseph knew he was breaking the rules. He was touching the artwork, breathing on it, stepping on it. But now, he had found a reason why he should be so close to the artwork.

He examined the ceiling with his flashlight. There was no sign of a leak, no pipe, no stain, no drip. He shined the flashlight onto the statue. There was clearly water there.

Joseph climbed onto the pedestal base of the statues. The bead of water looked like a teardrop. He put his index finger into the droplet. He pulled it away and rubbed the water with his thumb and index finger. He brought the finger up to his own eyes and looked at the wetness glistening in the dim light. He opened his mouth and placed the tip of his finger on his tongue. It was salty.

He thought he would need to report this. Yes, he definitely would. He had found water on a priceless statue. Joseph stepped off the pedestal and looked at the scene, the lovers trying to reach one another, the man defaced with no head or left hand. Joseph's gaze locked on the man's wrist. He felt a pain in his own hand. He sighed quietly. "I feel your pain, old fella. Wish I could have stopped the people who broke your hand and head off. That wouldn't have happened on my watch."

He rotated his wrist. His whole hand was really hurting. He rubbed his wrist with his right hand. He let out a moan, which alarmed him. It was a sickly cry in the quiet of the night.

Now he felt a pressure in his neck. He massaged the back of his neck to relieve the tension. Joseph tried to walk, but the pain stopped him and took his breath away. He couldn't breathe.

Falling to the wooden floor, landing on his back, the pain in his hand felt like a clamp was severing it. He writhed in pain and lay helpless on his back. As he stared at the ceiling, a gruesome sight appeared. It was a hand, dripping with blood floating through the air, moving toward the statues.

His neck, his neck, it felt like it was being broken. He couldn't move. He couldn't swallow. He couldn't breathe. But he could hear snapping and gurgling.

His gaze slowly became elevated. He saw down the hall. He looked at the other statues so nicely laid out in a row.

His vision moved to the floor. It was as if he was in a dream. He saw a body lying on the floor. He saw blood, blood leaking from the body. The body had no head and was missing a hand. It was wearing his clothes.

Now he could see her. She was coming into his vision. His gaze was locked upon her beautiful, stone face.

His hand was reaching for her.

The lights in the gallery went dark.

But he could see through the darkness that her expression was changing, her eyes narrowing, and her smile becoming a smirk.

It was as if she was saying, "I have you now. You're mine, and you are not going anywhere."

The dead of night silenced the room.

Into the Light

It is true that I am the youngest branch manager at Your Trust Savings and Loan. Gaining this title was not an honor. It was a set up for failure.

Perhaps they promoted me to branch manager simply because I wasn't paying attention. Stories of unexplained open drawers meant nothing to me.

Our savings and loan has six locations. My branch is the oldest but smallest. I have two employees. Three, if I count the janitorial service.

After I became manager, I did notice something strange with the curtains one day. They were swaying like they were being blown by the wind. I remember being puzzled as it occurred to me that the window was permanently locked. I looked around and noticed that there was no air conditioning vent in the area.

Standing next to the curtain, watching it billow in and out, I wondered what could be doing this. There didn't seem to be any airflow around it. I brought my hand to the curtain and held it.

The curtain stopped moving for a moment. Then I felt a tremendous tug as the whole curtain shot upward, ripping it from my hand. I fell backwards and nearly ended up on the floor. I stared at the curtain. Once again, it began to gently flow back and forth.

I asked Susan and Connor, my tellers, if they had ever witnessed anything like this. Connor nodded his head as Susan answered, "Yes, it happens nearly every day. It is best to ignore it."

"Why?"

"Because you can't stop it, and if you try, bad things happen."

"Like what?"

Susan sighed. "I don't want to say, but please, just accept it. Treat it as business as usual."

About a week later, after I had locked all the doors at closing, I came into my office and noticed that every drawer in my desk had been opened. I was alone. I had just been in my office. How could the drawers have been opened?

I walked through the office and checked behind the counter. I tugged on the back door. I saw nothing unusual, but then I discovered that the two front doors, which I had just locked, were now wide open.

Although they were designed to always swing shut, the doors were staying open. I walked over to them and closed them. Pulling out my keys, I relocked them. I double-checked to make sure they were indeed locked.

I didn't call the police. What could I say? "I locked the doors and then they were open. The drawers in my desk were pulled out."

That night, cleaning up after my dinner, I had an epiphany. The stories were true. There was a ghost at my branch. Susan had been telling me that there was nothing I could do about it.

Up until this point, the fact that one of the previous branch managers had been locked in the vault and nearly died of fright had seemed an unfortunate accident.

Then I remembered another branch manager had broken her arm and ankle on a nasty fall down the steps into the basement. Perhaps she was not merely clumsy?

I was the manager of a haunted savings and loan. My stomach churned. I hadn't learned about this in business school, but I would take the time to figure out what to do.

The bank was quiet for a week. Just as my hopes were up one afternoon, I heard a noise coming from my office. It was a metallic sound, like a rolling metal dish. I went into the office and found my coat rack rolling on the middle of the floor.

Following Susan's advice, I said, "That's my ghost," and went back to my work.

Another quiet week went by and then at closing time we were having trouble reconciling accounts. One stack of bills was $20 short. My teller rechecked one of the other stacks that had already been counted but found it to be $20 over. So we put the $20 with the short stack and double-checked that it was right, but it was now $20 over.

While the two stacks of $1,000 each were on the counter, something unbelievable happened right in front of our eyes. Susan and I saw it. This is true. I am not exaggerating. One of the $20 bills was sliding across the counter, going from one stack to the other.

Then those two stacks began to spread out on the counter. The bills began to rise up into the air and then fall down onto the counter. I lurched at the falling bills and stuffed them into a bag. I put the bag into the vault and locked the big door. Susan and I practically ran out of the bank.

I was shivering. I said to Susan, "I don't know if I can take this."

She said to me, "You can't fight it, or bad things will

happen to you. That is what happened to the other managers. Gus was cursing at the ghost when he got locked into the vault. Emily was trying to lock it downstairs when she fell down the steps."

"I have to do something," I said.

"Well, don't do what they did," she warned.

After I started up my car, I had trouble putting it into gear. My nerves were shot. I was near tears. I was worried that this ghost was in the car with me.

I managed to get home. That Friday night, I drifted in and out of a restless, fearful sleep. On Saturday, I had the day off and gradually relaxed. I had been doing some reading on ghosts, and I increased my research trying to find out what others had done in similar situations. Through my study, I formed a plan to stop this ghost from haunting my branch. I was going to need to go into the bank basement.

Sunday afternoon, I opened up the back door to go into my branch. The building was 115 years old. I paused for a moment. How many stories were there about the very threshold I was walking over?

Once inside, I opened the door to the basement where we kept our archives. I walked down the wooden stairs confident I was doing the right thing. As I descended the steps, I was overcome with the eerie feeling that I was now in the very place that my ghost lurked. I switched on the single, bare light bulb that hung from the ceiling in this small, musty basement.

Walking to the metal bookshelf, I pulled out the big album of newspaper clippings. This book contained every article that mentioned our branch in the first 90 years of its existence. I took the book over to the round table next to the wall.

I began to search for information about someone who had died at our bank, someone who was now haunting our branch, someone who had been long forgotten.

After two hours of searching, my heart began to pound harder as I read the following story:

Homeless Farmer Dies Near Savings & Loan

Robert Cole was found frozen to death yesterday morning. His body was discovered in the alley behind the Savings and Loan.

It was an ironic death for the once prosperous farmer to die on the back steps of this institution. Years ago, he had claimed to have brought in more than $4,000 on the day of the infamous bank run, the day that the Savings and Loan managed to stay open, while the other banks in town were forced to close.

Cole had said that he had given his money to the manager Sven Johanson, who died from a heart attack that very night. According to Cole, his money was the reason Johanson was able to keep the Savings and Loan open. Cole said that because he and Johanson were friends, and because of the turmoil that day, he never got a receipt.

When the next branch manager refused to believe Cole's story, Cole lost his farm in bankruptcy. Recently, he had been homeless. Cole will be buried in the paupers' field.

My mouth was dry as I finished reading this story. I said to the empty, dingy basement, "Mr. Cole, are you here now?" A moment later, I felt a sensation of cold touch my hand. I swallowed hard and said, "I can hardly imagine what it would be like to freeze to death on the back steps of the very institution that took your money." I felt that same cold sensation on the front of my throat and then the back of my neck. "Mr. Cole, it's time for you to go."

Suddenly, there was a pressure on my throat. I began to have trouble breathing. I managed to say, "Mr. Cole, your business is done here. You need to leave."

At this point, the pressure on my throat was so great I

could scarcely breathe, and I fell off my chair to the floor. I uttered, "Mr. Cole, I will get a plaque, and on the plaque..." I was gasping for air. "On the plaque, I will mount the newspaper story. I will title the plaque, 'The True Story of the Man Who Saved Our Savings and Loan.' Mr. Cole, I believe you."

When I said this, the pressure was slowly released from my throat. As I sucked in air, I started to see a blue light radiating from a figure crouched next to me. As I stared in amazement, I said, "Mr. Cole, I apologize on behalf of all of the past managers who did not believe you. I thank you for what you did for our Savings and Loan. I will honor you."

Now, I saw the crouched figure with the blue light stand up and move toward the center of the room. The blue light began to change hues. It went from dark blue to light blue to aqua blue. It began to flicker and sparkle. The blue figure stood beneath the white light of the bare light bulb.

The white light and the blue light began to grow in intensity. They became so bright, I could no longer look at them. I turned away, but I could see them flashing and merging on the wall, the blue and white coming together.

There was then a tremendous explosion that sounded like one toll of a gigantic, metal bell. BONNNG.

And then I was engulfed in darkness. My ears were ringing, but soon a silence settled into that room. And I lay on the floor in the dark listening to the silence. A sense of peace came over me. I laid there for at least a minute, and then I got up, walked through the dark of the room, and carefully climbed up the stairs into the light of the Savings and Loan. The very next day, I ordered the plaque to honor Mr. Cole.

Going Down

It could be said that alcohol was at least partially responsible. The drinks were flowing all night for the celebration.

Whatever the case, when the CEO of Your Shocking Friend, Inc. walked up to the podium, there was a standing ovation before he even said a word.

Bennett Kirk had transformed his company. In the last 12 years, he had taken it from a two-person startup to the powerhouse of the defibrillation industry. His company was outselling all of their competitors combined.

It was profitable work. This celebration was a reward night and at the same time designed to pump up his sales team to keep dominating the market.

After he had talked for a few minutes, he told them, "Do

you know what a ghost is? A ghost is that little voice in your head that tries to keep you from being your best, that fills you with doubt."

He took a sip of his beer and smiled at the team. "Well, I am here tonight to put another voice in your head. Don't let the bastards get you down." There was huge applause and cheers.

Bennett laughed. "That's right, when you have challenges, when you run into people who are roadblocks to your success, my voice is going to echo in your head. Don't let the bastards get you down." Bennett pumped his fist in the air shouting, "Let's have our best year ever!" He nodded to the band, and they immediately started playing the fast section of "Stairway to Heaven." Every person in the room jumped back on their feet as the place exploded with applause.

There was one person in the room, though, who wasn't applauding. He had been standing next to Bennett during the speech, occasionally whispering something in his ear.

The next day, the most memorable thing from the night before was a hangover. Bennett was jetting across the country to an evening fundraiser. He was trying to clear his head and focus. He was glad there was a corporate jet so that he didn't have to talk to anyone else. He was best when he made his decisions without interference.

The man from the night before was seated at his side. The man leaned over and said to Bennett, "You know what day it is, and you act like you don't care."

Bennett knew that it was his daughter's 10th birthday. He was going to miss her party. He had pressing business obligations. He couldn't be there for every little family function.

"You haven't seen her in six months," the man said.

Bennett exhaled hard. "I call her all the time," he thought.

"You haven't talked to her in more than a month."

Bennett took a drink from his seltzer water. Tonight, in Seattle, he had a chance to really make a difference. He had big plans for his company, and he was in the business of saving lives. Nothing was going to stop him.

New markets were his specialty. He had learned that there was no better way to open up a market than to have mandated regulation. Bennett's current emphasis was to get a series of units in every high school sports stadium in the country.

To achieve this, he had to be able to tug on heartstrings. To do that, he had learned a long time ago that he needed to really care about the people he wanted to help. Every kid who collapsed at a sporting event was a poster child for his company, but was also fuel for Bennett's own sadness. Bennett had learned of a state legislator whose daughter had died on a soccer field. Your Shocking Friend, Inc. was about to make a large donation to that representative and was going to suggest language for a state bill that could save young lives every year. It was more than a marketing technique for Bennett. It was his calling to make a difference in the world.

The man sitting next to Bennett was no stranger. He had been with Bennett since the beginning. He continued to whisper, "Will it ever be enough? Why are you really doing this?"

Bennett tried to focus on the business at hand. He told himself, "This isn't about making money. We are trying to save lives."

The whisper came again, "Yes, business is good, and you are helping people, but what about your daughter, and your wife?"

The divorce happened five years ago. Bennett could visit his daughter every weekend if he had time. But he didn't. One day, his daughter could join the company. One day, all of this would be hers.

Bennett thought about his daughter who would be having a pool party today at the house. He pictured her practicing her backflip into the pool.

A business thought forced its way in front of his musings about his daughter. He had hopes of legislation that would require a defibrillator in every home that had a swimming pool. In his mind, every person who died in a pool was "the reason for my non-stop work." He rephrased his thought, "one death too many."

The man sitting next to Bennett was considering an intervention. Whispering wasn't enough. Bennett was exceptionally bright but didn't seem to understand that there was more than one way to lose a life. The man sitting by Bennett was Jacob Grow, cofounder of Your Shocking Friend, Inc. He was Bennett's best man at his wedding. Since Jacob died eight years ago, Bennett wasn't listening to him. The pressure of the business consumed Bennett's attention.

Jacob was a businessman, too. It was time to leverage the situation.

His lifeless body floated up the aisle and entered through the cockpit door without opening it. He took control of the plane. It began to rapidly descend. The helpless pilot tried to correct the plunging aircraft, but there was nothing he could do.

Bennett's drink was on the floor. "My god, what the hell is the matter?"

"I don't know, sir."

From 33,000 feet to 20,000 feet, Bennett thought about how this was going to interrupt his plans for the evening.

From 20,000 feet to 15,000 feet, Bennett tried to help the pilot.

From 15,000 to 5,000 feet, Bennett's life flashed before him, who he was, where he had come from, and whom he had always loved. His daughter was foremost in his mind. A dozen pictures of who she was and what she meant to him ripped a hole in his heart and then restarted it.

From 5,000 to 2,000, Bennett prayed for his life. He pledged that if he made it through this alive, he would change. He would be there for his daughter. He would apologize to his ex-wife. He would not live his life only for business.

From 2,000 to 1,500, he swore that he would be true to his word. "I promise. I promise. I promise."

The plane righted itself, roaring over a cornfield, and began climbing.

"I don't know what happened, sir, but I am heading to the nearest airport. It is Springfield, Illinois."

"Springfield?" asked Bennett with a quiver.

"Yes, sir."

That was his hometown, where the birthday party was today. Trembling, Bennett imagined arriving at the house for his daughter's celebration. Could he actually show up? Would he be welcome?

He closed his eyes. Tears made their way out of his closed lids and ran down his cheeks.

"Don't worry, old buddy," Jacob said, while putting his hand on Bennett's shoulder. "It's all going to work out."

Dead Wrong

It was the last Friday of the month and the team was not getting along. It was 12:02 p.m., and they had cancelled their plans to eat together.

Kim opened the door to get out of their office, but before she could get through the doorway, the door slammed shut. Kim put her hand back on the doorknob, but it wouldn't turn. "Dang," she said.

"Let me do it," said Paul. The five of them were clustered in a group at the door.

"Paul, shut up. It's really stuck here." Kim pulled on the door again. Then they switched places. Paul grunted. The door didn't budge.

They were the portfolio management team for one of

the most successful mutual funds their company offered. They shared a corner office on the 12th floor.

"Well, let's call security," said Kim.

Shonda said, "I'll do it." She picked up one of the phones and pushed the talk button. There was no tone. "The phone is not working."

"That's crazy," Serge said. "First the door, now the phone. I'll just send an email."

"That's stupid. I'll call on my cell phone," said Mary. She pulled it out of her purse but dropped it. The screen shattered on the floor. "Oh, crap."

"Computers aren't working," said Serge.

Kim had her cell phone in her hand now. She was looking up the number for building security. The phone came out of her hand. It went flying through the air as if it had been thrown and crashed into one of the walls.

The crash startled everybody. Mary let out a muffled scream. Shonda said, "What the hell."

Paul's phone slipped out of his pocket and rose up into the air. He noticed it and grabbed it. "What's going on? That didn't just happen…I can't hold this. It's killing my fingers." He let go and the phone broke apart in mid air and fell to the ground.

Shonda's purse started rocking. The strap was over her shoulder. The purse turned upside down and spilt the contents. Her phone hadn't broken, but now it was spinning on the floor. Then, like a jet, it shot across the room crashing into a metal cabinet. The phone shattered into pieces.

Mary was on the ground looking at her cell phone pieces. She crawled over to Serge's computer. "Why won't it work?" she shouted. Serge tried to get something on the screen. His chair started to shake. He held onto the armrests, but the chair tipped to the floor with him in it. He moaned, "No, no, I want this to stop."

Now Serge's phone holster was unsnapped. He looked down at his hip and saw his phone rise into the air and then shoot up into the florescent ceiling light. A mixture of glass and plastic fell to the floor.

"Crap, glass is in my hair," Shonda screamed.

One of the shades on the window lowered itself. It went up and down and back up. It began moving up and down in some kind of pattern.

"Holy shit," Kim said in disbelief.

"The shades," said Shonda. "They are doing the SOS signal. Three short, three long, then three short."

The shades stopped. Shonda whispered, "I got a really bad feeling about this." She sniffled and wiped her nose with the back of her hand.

A box of Kleenex rose up from the table. One sheet came out, and the box fell to the floor. The tissue danced its way through the air and landed on the floor next to a box of paperclips that had come out of Shonda's purse.

The box opened and a paperclip floated into the air. It began to straighten itself out. Now the tissue was back in the air, skirting the ground. The two objects moved across the floor to underneath Serge's desk. The paperclip went into one of the open sockets on the power strip with a series of sparks. The tissue came to rest upon it.

The team watched with their mouths open, their eyes fixed on this unbelievable sight. The tissue burst into flames and burned itself out in a yellow blaze.

The shades started moving again. Long, short, long, long. Long, long, long. Short, short, long.

"Y, O, U," said Shonda.

Paul asked, "How do you know that?"

"It's Morse code, just like the SOS." The shade continued to go up and down. Shonda called out the letters.

"A, R, E, D, E, A, D."

Kim shrieked, "You are dead."

Mary whimpered. Serge was biting his knuckles. Paul went back to the door and began to pull with all his might.

The shades continued.

Shonda called out the letters. "W, R, O, N, G, A, N, D, S, T, U, P, I, D." The shades stopped moving.

"You are dead wrong and stupid." Kim half laughed as she put it all together.

They all knew who used that phrase. Serge asked the question, "Could Mack be here?"

Their boss, Mack, had died six weeks earlier. One of his favorite phases was "dead wrong and stupid." It was his description of what happened to people who didn't think through their research.

Mack's philosophy was that you needed the algorithms, but you had to put the pieces together yourself, and no one person could do it all. It took a team to do it right. Since he was gone, the team did not have a manager. They were operating on a joint leadership model, consensus based.

But today had been a disaster. No one had been listening to anyone else.

Another tissue went over to the paperclip in the power strip, then another. With each tissue, more smoke filled the room.

"Could this be a test?" Kim blurted out.

"Maybe," said Serge. "Maybe Mack is trying to make us act like a team. He could be upset with us because we used the phrase 'good enough' today."

"Those were your words," Paul said accusingly.

"Yeah, but we all agreed to it," Kim said.

"We didn't agree on anything," Paul retorted.

Serge tried to get back on his computer. "It doesn't seem to have power."

"We need help to get out of here," Kim said. "Maybe we could lower a sign to the floor below us."

"We don't have any string to lower it with," said Shonda.

One of the tall cabinets in the office began to rock and then fell over. Mary was nearly hit, but at the last second Paul had dived to her, pushing her out of the way.

Kim yelled, "We got to get out of here." Then, looking up

at the ceiling she called out, "I am sorry, boss, please just let us go."

Shonda was trembling. "What if we use Morse Code?" She looked at the others.

Mary asked, "Use Morse Code on what? The shades? Who is going to see that?"

Serge said, "Knowing Mack, he wants us to do something together."

"That makes sense," Shonda said. "But what?"

"Oh shit, look at that," Paul pointed. A pair of scissors was moving through the air. It was opening and closing. It was above Kim. It started to cut her hair. She tried to run, but the scissors followed.

Mary pulled off her coat and captured the scissors in it. She took the bundle to the supply closet, tossed it in, and shut the door.

Their boss, Mack, had gotten colon cancer. He had told them it was because they were such a pain in the ass. He was unconventional, a mix of old-school research and big-data programming. Use the data, but let the mind process it.

Paul said, "What if we pound out the SOS on the door until someone hears us."

"No one will hear because the other units on our floor are off site today," Mary said.

"And who is going to know what it means, anyway?" Kim said.

Paul jumped in, "They don't have to know what it means. They just have to hear it and respond to the knocking."

"Yeah," said Serge. "Let's jump up and down on the floor."

"Let's all do it together." Mary pleaded.

"That will bring the people from programing up here. We know that works. Remember the party last year?" Kim asked.

The remaining lights went out. The room grew dim.

Shonda started jumping up and down. Three quick jumps, then three slow jumps, then three quick jumps. They all joined in.

"Let's yell, too," said Mary.

They did. "Ah, ah, ah, aaaaaah, aaaaaah, aaaaaah, ah, ah, ah."

Five minutes later, the door was being opened.

They fell into a massive group hug. As they looked in each other's eyes, they burst out laughing. Then Mary started crying.

"Let's go out to lunch together," Shonda said. Everyone agreed. They would clean up the mess later.

Although they never heard from their former boss again, the message stuck. Every time one of them put the shades up or down, the whole team would shout, "Mack, we hear you loud and clear."

Number One

Paul Edmondson could actually see the voice of Jan Choe traveling through the telephone wire. He saw a spot in the line that was thin and put his ghostly finger on it.

Choe's call was interrupted with static.

Edmondson began to laugh and pulled his finger away from the wire. The static stopped, and Choe continued talking. He put his finger back on the line. The static came back. Choe said in a loud voice, "Sorry, I can't make out what you are saying. I'll try to call back."

Edmondson had worked himself to death. He had been the number one salesperson for 18 of the last 26 months, beating Choe and the other staff members month after month.

It was the end of March and his numbers had been

slightly off so he had been trying his hardest to close a couple of deals to ensure that he would remain number one.

When he was behind, he could hardly stand it. In his mind, he was nothing if he wasn't number one.

Choe had been in the lead this month. She was confident, persistent, perceptive, and especially good at listening to find out what her customers wanted.

Edmondson had caught a cold, which turned out to be the flu. He soldiered through it, taking pills to keep his fever down and his headache at bay. But when he threw up in the office restroom, his boss told him to go home, that he looked like the walking dead.

Edmondson refused and worked late that night. His efforts paid off. He closed another deal and was back on top. He passed out from exhaustion at his desk. No one was there to notice. He died in his sleep.

The night janitor found him.

Jan Choe had one more day to take the top sales position that month.

Even in death, Paul Edmondson wanted to stay on top. He ignored the invitation to the light and stayed in the dark office waiting for the staff to arrive.

He had a job to do. He was going to stop Choe from taking his place as top salesperson.

Jan was shaken by Paul's death. She spent the morning in a kind of daze. She volunteered to get flowers to send to Paul's sister. But now in the afternoon, she had to get herself together and do her job. She was making a call confirming an appointment when the ghost of Edmondson had struck.

Choe tried to call back, but once again there was too much static.

Choe picked up her cell phone and dialed the number.

Edmondson could see the cell phone signal. He opened his mouth and swallowed the call.

Choe said, "Damn, what's going on with the stupid phones?"

Now she was in her car driving over to her first appointment. Paul Edmondson was sitting in the passenger seat without his seatbelt buckled. He wasn't worried about getting in an accident. He was hoping for one. He inserted his hand into the steering column and shorted the ignition circuit. The car died.

Choe pulled over to the side of the road. "Now what?"

When Choe tried to restart her car, it wouldn't even turn over. "You've got to be kidding." She squeezed the steering wheel with both hands. She shut her eyes for a moment and then got out of the car and walked up to the next street. Choe hailed a cab. Edmondson got in with her.

Forty-five minutes later, it looked like Choe was closing a deal. She opened her order tablet. Her client was nodding his head. Edmondson was also in the building trying to stop the deal. The smoke alarm went off. That piercing tone stopped all conversation. The sprinklers came on.

This was a disaster for the office. Choe's client would have to talk to her another day.

Ten minutes later, Edmondson watched Choe as they rode in the cab to another sales client. Choe looked frustrated, tired, and wet. "Good," he said to himself.

Choe went in the building for her next call. She got into the elevator alone. It stopped before she reached her floor. Choe waited. She re-pushed the button for the 20th floor. A minute passed. She pressed the alarm button. The bell rang. A long time passed.

At 12 minutes to five the elevator started working again. Choe got off at the 20th floor and rushed to talk to her client. She learned he had just left for the day.

Choe decided to call it a day. She had dinner out and then went back to her apartment. Edmondson was watching her. She was defeated. She wasn't number one this month. He was looking forward to feeding on her despair, her depression, her sense of loss.

Yet, she wasn't giving him what he wanted.

She called a friend and told her about her day and about

the unfortunate death of her co-worker. Jan had mentioned that she was not going to be the number one salesperson this month. She added, "You can't win them all."

Now Jan was lounging on her couch with a glass of wine in her hand, music playing, and a soft light coming from her dragonfly lamp.

She wasn't crying. She wasn't hitting her fist against the wall. She wasn't throwing up her supper.

She wasn't doing any of the things Edmondson had done when he wasn't number one.

She was relaxing on her couch listening to music.

Edmondson could hardly look at her. He wanted her to feel the loss of not being number one.

Edmondson stopped the music.

Jan didn't even get up to check it.

The light went out.

Jan got up, but she didn't try the light switch. She just opened a drawer and pulled out matches. She lit a candle and got back on the couch.

Edmondson wanted that light out. He tried to extinguish the candle, but he didn't have any breath.

Her breathing was steady, and she closed her eyes.

The flickering light from the candle caught Edmondson's attention. He put his finger on the base of the candle and moved it across the table. He could push the candle into the dried flowers, which were also in an arrangement on the table. He could cause a fire and block the door shut. Then Choe would suffer like she should.

He wanted her to suffer like he had all those months that he had not been number one. Why was she relaxing?

It was then that Edmondson had an unexpected thought. "She is better than me. She deserved to win."

The candle flickered in the darkness. It beckoned.

He put his face right next to it and stared at it. The light stimulated his thoughts. There was something more important than being number one. It was a quality that Jan exhibited. It allowed her to be OK even when things didn't go her way.

"I've seen enough," Paul said. His body shifted as he relaxed. A white aura started to surround him as he began to glow in the darkened room.

The spirit of Paul Edmondson put his glowing index finger into the fire. It was as if two flames were coming together. His finger was soon gone and then his whole hand, followed by his arm. He dropped his head into the flickering light. The flame flared up and crackled. It enveloped his spirit and drew the rest of his ghostly body into the tiny blaze.

He embraced the light. He left Jan Choe.

Jan opened her eyes just as the music came back on, and the dragonfly lamp relit. She said to herself, "Tomorrow will be a better day."

Bridge

Dressed in a brown suit, Blake Touhy took a step onto the haunted bridge. It was a covered pedestrian walkway connecting marketing with manufacturing. It was rarely used.

The 100-year-old ornate metal door that Blake opened was a reminder of the long-term success of the company. The bridge was totally enclosed and had tinted windows on both sides. It spanned about 100 yards with large pipes and wires that ran along its length. In the late-afternoon sun, it had an eerie darkness to it.

Blake's wing-tipped shoes shuffled as he walked along the bridge. He wondered if he would see "the lady."

Once a month, someone from the marketing department would walk to the manufacturing plant to advise the supervisors of the upcoming sales projections. Of course, marketing could have simply sent an email, but the VP felt it best to add a personal touch. "Tell people in person what you need them to do," she said.

There were stories from some of the other marketing folks who had walked this bridge by themselves. They had said that there was a lady who appeared to them. They said she was a ghost. They also said they wouldn't go back on that bridge.

Blake loosened his yellow tie just a bit. He didn't believe in ghosts, but this bridge was like a dim tunnel, and it gave him the creeps. Plus, he was nervous about telling manufacturing what he needed them to do. "Sometimes people don't want to listen," he thought.

He made it to the other side. Blake opened the wooden door and entered the plant for his meeting. Once he and the supervisor sat down, Blake said, "Over the next two months, sales will be exceptionally high because of the discounts we are advertising." Blake handed him the sales forecast.

The supervisor looked over the sheet and shook his head. "These numbers are unrealistic. We don't have enough staff to produce this volume. Why don't you ever ask us before you launch your advertising campaigns?"

Blake responded, "Look, we have our job, and you have your job. We work hard to make our advertising dollars go as far as possible. Opportunities come up quickly, and we have to take advantage of them. That is what pays my salary, and that is what pays your salary. The plan is already in motion. I'm sorry, but end of discussion."

As Blake started the walk back to his building across the bridge, he wondered why the manufacturing people didn't seem to understand how the business worked. Why couldn't they be excited at the prospect of accelerating production? It meant overtime for them, and extra staff could be hired. The more people working the better, Blake thought.

He looked up and was startled to see someone else on the bridge. A woman was standing ahead of him. Like many of the plant workers, the woman was dressed in coveralls. As Blake walked by her, the woman said in a gravelly voice, "You have no idea."

Blake didn't say anything, didn't look back. As he walked, he thought, "This must be the lady." To muster his courage, he closed his eyes and clenched his fists for a brief second.

Twenty feet further, Blake saw the woman again. Blake wondered how she had gotten ahead of him. As Blake approached, she frowned and said in a voice so quiet Blake could barely hear it, "You have no idea."

Blake blurted out, "What? What do I have no idea about?"

The woman shook her head in disgust.

Blake stopped walking and looked closer at this lady. Blake seemed to be seeing through her. Blake could see the pipes that were behind the woman.

An intense fear rippled through Blake. He took one step backwards. The woman turned away from him and began to crank a metal wheel attached to one of the pipes. Mist spread across the bridge.

The white mist filled the passageway so that Blake could no longer see the door to marketing. Trembling, Blake walked into the steamy mist. A few steps later, the woman appeared in his path.

Blake shouted out, "Leave me alone."

It was a face-to-face moment of marketing being stopped by manufacturing. The woman was scowling at him. She disappeared into the mist. All Blake could hear was the hissing of the steam and his own labored breathing.

The corridor went totally white. After a moment, Blake saw a patch of color up ahead. It was like a little movie playing. The mist was the screen. He saw in this picture a meeting was taking place. A man in a suit was saying, "It has to be this material on the product. It's what sells!"

A man in a blue shirt was saying, "It's not possible to use that material. It doesn't matter if it sells. The compounds involved are toxic. It is not safe."

"Do your job, and use the material. Make it safe! That's your job."

A new scene appeared in the mist. Blake saw a pipe coming out of a concrete wall. The pipe was discharging liquid into a pond. All the while, the manufacturing plant was in the background.

At first, frogs were jumping, croaking, and swimming in the pond. Then floating on the water, decaying with flies buzzing above them. The buzzing got louder, and louder, and then stopped abruptly.

An organ began to play. Blake saw a stained-glassed window. People crying. A coffin with the lid closed. Screams of grief filled the bridge. Then the pictures were gone, and the corridor went silent, except for the hissing of the steam.

Blake stumbled over to the glass window and looked down. Leaning against the glass wall, he could barely make out the ground. He needed to get off this bridge. He forced himself to continue to walk toward the marketing building. Because of the mist, he couldn't see his feet, which was disorienting, like he wasn't fully there.

Blake heard someone breathing behind him and then a voice: "You have no idea. We have seen your kind before."

Blake turned to where he had heard the voice. No one was there. As he turned back, color shone in the white mist, once again. He saw a vision of a meeting between two men. A man in a suit was saying, "The plant has to do better. You have to keep up with the sales forecast. The success of our quarterly earnings rests upon it."

"It's not safe. It pushes our workers too hard."

Words came out in slow motion from the man in the suit. "You will do it. Your job is on the line. Find a way."

Blake then saw in the mist an image of a giant sorting wall, dropping containers to the belt below. It was a white incline with a never-ending tumble of containers going to the belt.

As the scene continued, Blake watched a woman at the

top of the incline. She was trying to free a stuck container. The woman loses her balance, slips, tries to stay on her feet, slides down the incline, screams, slips some more, hits the solid pole by the belt. Red everywhere. The woman is caught in the bottom of the belt and wedged against the pole.

Blake was sick. Sweat poured off his forehead. He couldn't breathe. He fell to his knees and began to crawl through the mist toward the metal doors that led to the marketing department.

As he crawled, Blake's hand came down next to a boot. He saw a leg. The woman leaned down. Her face appeared. The face transformed before Blake's eyes. It was now covered in blood. The woman stepped back. Her stomach, her legs, her boots were all covered in blood.

She disappeared into the white, steaming mist. Blake let out a choked cry. He realized that the visions he had seen were of the bleak history of his successful company. He knew there were manufacturing deaths. He knew there were chemical spills and lawsuit payoffs.

A flash of yellow up ahead, then brown, another colored scene gradually appeared. Blake stopped and watched it. This was someone in a suit lying on a floor crying for help. "Help me. Help. Heeelp."

Gradually, the picture came into focus and revealed the man's face. It was Blake.

He yelled, "Stop it."

Blake now saw in the mist the meeting room he had been in. He saw the plant supervisor, who was shaking his head. He was saying, "These numbers are unrealistic. We don't have enough staff to produce this volume."

Blake watched and listened to himself say, "This is what pays your salary. The plan is already in motion. I'm sorry, but end of discussion." The picture faded. The mist in the tunnel began to swirl.

In the heat of the enclosed tunnel, Blake forced himself to crawl toward the door. His face felt like it was blistering. He collapsed to the ground. Now he was on his belly, creeping like a baby, still trying to make his way to the door.

The steam was scalding his hands. Blake felt his lungs burning.

The door, the door, he must make it to the door.

He stopped, let out another cry. "Help me! Help. Heeelp."

On the floor, stuck in the mist, he gasped. Those were the very words he had just heard. He felt he must be in a dream. He was scooting his way through a scalding nightmare.

He touched the door. He had made it. He managed to stand. He pulled the door handle. It wouldn't open.

Blake pounded on the door. He pounded and pounded for what seemed a full minute. He lost his strength and fell back to his knees. He collapsed in a ball.

The woman in the coveralls appeared to him in the mist. She bent down and whispered in his ear. "Now you have an idea of the other side."

Like the steam clearing in the room, the lady went from visible to invisible.

Deadbeats

Sue Their Ass Legal Associates seemed like a great firm. I was thrilled to get a job in their physical evidence department.

My team sorted through the various documents, reports, and notes that were not in electronic form. I became the seventh member of a group affectionately known as the Deadbeats.

The Deadbeats got their name because they almost never seemed busy. The thing was, they got their work done very quickly. After that, they could do anything they wanted.

On my second day there, our team received about 10 boxes of medical files. We were to read through them, tab and highlight key sections, and write a series of summaries. They gave me about 300 pages.

At the end of the day, I was on page 207 and the rest of

the Deadbeats were playing poker. Somehow, they had finished the rest of the 10 boxes.

"How did you do it?" I asked. "How did you get through that much material accurately and quickly?"

Jose, Susan, Jeff, Yolanda, Kiefer, and Sam looked at me at the same time. It was both comical and creepy. They started to laugh.

Kiefer said, "We have superhuman skills."

Susan said, "Do you want to be one of us?"

"Yeah," I said.

"All you have to do," said Susan, "is a short flight, a tiny swallow, or take the big plunge."

"What does that mean?"

They laughed again. I still had 100 pages to go, and they were playing cards. And now they were laughing at me.

Susan said, "There will be plenty of chances to join us, but for now just get your work done the old fashioned way, by the sweat of your brow!"

I finished my 300 pages and the summary statements a little bit before noon the next day. The Deadbeats were headed out to lunch.

Jose invited me to join the group. "Come on, big fella! Come celebrate with us."

My lunch was in the refrigerator. "No, I am going to stay in the office this time. I already have my lunch here."

"Party pooper, party pooper," Yolanda sang out.

They got in the elevator at 11:55 and didn't get back to the office until 3:20. They clearly had been drinking.

Jeff put his arm around me. "All work and no play make Gavin a very dull boy. Next time you've got to come out with us, dude." He rubbed the top of my head with his knuckles.

I had been reading a series of briefs that had been sent to our work group. We had work to do, but they said it could wait until tomorrow morning.

"We will do it in the morning, and since it will be Friday, we will have a dart tournament in the afternoon," Jeff said.

"No, I don't think so," I said. "They have just delivered 20 boxes to us."

"Holy crap," said Yolanda. "We better get started right away, or we will have to work all weekend."

They burst out laughing. Kiefer turned on the TV, and they began to watch "Judge Judy."

Susan looked at me watching them. She walked over to me. "Why don't you just pick a box and get started? Don't worry about us. You'll see. It will all get done in the morning."

As I headed to my office with my box, I started to wonder if this job would be like the rest of my life. As a kid, my family moved nine times before I was 15 years old. I never had time to make friends, or be comfortable with the people around me. I was determined to fit in with the Deadbeats.

I worked until 7 p.m. that night. It was a 12-hour day for me, and four of those hours were time and a half. The rest of my team had left at 4:30. "Shhh," they said in unison as they left.

They were done with the 19 boxes before lunch. I was barely into my box. I imagined that they didn't read anything. I didn't know what they did; yet, I did know that they were known as the most efficient and careful readers of the whole firm. I had asked to be part of this team. I loved to read and was great at analysis, but I was clearly missing something here.

Friday night, I worked past dinner. The Deadbeats had left at 4:45 after a raucous afternoon of dart playing and beer pong. As I was reading at my desk, a bit before 8, I heard laughter. I stopped reading and listened. It seemed to be coming from outside. I stepped over to my office window. I saw lots of motion going through the air.

My jaw dropped wide enough to swallow a baseball. I knew what I was seeing, but I wouldn't let myself admit it. The Deadbeats were flying through the air, laughing and passing by the window. They were a ghostly grey and having the time of their lives, bumping into each other, high fiving, and turning somersaults.

As I looked out in disbelief, Susan flew to the window

and hovered in the air staring at me. She winked at me and flew off with the others.

I had no doubt I was hallucinating. I called it a night.

On Monday, as I was working through my box, Susan walked into my office and asked me, "So, how was your weekend?"

"It was good, very restful. I had worked late Friday night and needed some down time."

"My weekend was crazy fun. The Deadbeats are the best. It must seem strange to you how the rest of us 'fly' through our work."

The way she said "fly" gave me a chill. Was she telling me with a smile that I hadn't been hallucinating?

"Would you like to learn to 'fly' through your work the way we do?" she asked.

"What would I have to do?"

"Just take a short flight. Then you will be one of us."

"What do you mean a short flight?"

"You know," Susan said, "like, from the 8th floor to the ground."

I didn't know what to say to that. "I'm good. I'm just gonna keep working here."

"Suit yourself. But it is quick and easy and takes away all of your burdens."

Kiefer popped his head into my room, raised his eyebrows, and simultaneously put both thumbs up.

The next morning at 8, the Deadbeats were sitting around the circular table sipping their cappuccinos. I must admit that I love that wonderful mix of steamed milk and dark coffee, especially with a bit of flavoring in it.

Jose said, "Isn't this killer stuff?" He took a heaping spoonful of what appeared to be powdered chocolate and mixed it into his drink.

The Deadbeats passed the canister and spoon around the table, each taking a towering spoonful. Yolanda sprinkled the powder onto her drink. She brought the steaming cup up to her nose. "I live for this," she said.

I had my own caramel latté. I had joined them at the round table. Jeff handed me the canister. "Try some. Seriously, it is to die for."

I took the spoon and the canister in my hand. I turned the metal canister around and saw the words "rat poison" written on it. Everyone stared at me.

"Why does it say rat poison?"

"You know," Sam said, "we don't want to have any rats in the group." More laughing, or was it cackling?

"I think I'll pass."

"Come on," continued Sam, "just try one spoonful."

"What is it really?"

Susan smiled, "It's really good."

They were all looking at me, encouraging me to try some of the powder, nodding their heads up and down.

Awkward as it was, I put the canister down on the table. I got up and said, "Oh rats, I better get back to work." I walked out of the conference room. It was an awful feeling. I wanted to fit in, but I felt the team was playing me, like I was there for their amusement.

The next Wednesday, I had been working, and the Deadbeats were out for an extended lunch. When they came back, they were laughing and shouting. They called for me to come into the workroom.

"Guess what we learned how to do?" Yolanda said.

"It's dangerous," Sam warned.

"So you won't like it," Jeff stated.

"But we got you one anyway," Kiefer said.

"Please try it. Have some fun," Susan pleaded. I was impressed they had gotten me a gift.

Jose pulled out seven letter openers out of a wooden box. "These aren't actual swords, but they still work." Jose passed one of the letter openers to everybody but me.

"Let's all do it together," Sam said.

"You just watch," Susan said to me. "We learned this from a street performer at lunch."

The Deadbeats licked their letter openers, tilted back their heads, opened their mouths, and stuck the swords down their throats. They stretched out their arms in unison and wiggled their fingers for applause.

It was crazy impressive, and I applauded.

They pulled their swords out. "Now it's your turn," Susan said, handing me one of the short swords.

I felt the sides of my letter opener. It was sharp, more like a knife than a letter opener. "I am not doing that."

"Party pooper," sang Yolanda.

"Come on," Susan said. "Live a little."

"If you don't want to swallow it, try this," said Kiefer. He pulled his shirt out of his pants and unbuttoned the shirt. He thrust the letter opener into his exposed stomach. He partially opened his mouth and began to grunt as he moved the opener around in a rough circle. There was no blood. I thought it must be a trick knife, but I could see the opening in his cut skin. I could hear the cutting of flesh.

Kiefer removed his letter opener and pushed his other hand into the cut section of his stomach. As his fingers disappeared, I nearly passed out. The Deadbeats were falling over laughing.

"Give it a try," Susan said. "Do the deep plunge!"

"Join us, dude," Kiefer said. As I looked at them in horror, I saw something like sparks coming from their eyes.

"I got to go," I said to them. I put the letter opener down on the table. I walked out of our workroom and into the hallway, then up three flights of stairs. I was in a haze of confusion as I went to my manager's office. I knocked on his door.

"I need a new assignment. Can I work in the electronic forms division?"

My boss looked at me and frowned, "Why would you want to work with those little devils?"

Habits

Everything was on schedule after Bob's death. His resume had been accepted, his interview had gone well, and now it was time to return to his old job and get some answers.

On his first day back, the boss Gary Miller said to him, "By the way, if you want to look like a college kid, I think your hair is perfect. But if you want to step into the adult world, get a haircut."

Bob knew that the belittling comment about his hair was coming. It was his boss' way. Of course, no one at the company recognized Bob. He was old when he had died, and now he had taken on a younger form and a new name.

Mode Engineering did aeronautical contract work. It was a small firm, and this was a tiny team of four people.

It wasn't long before his co-worker Baxter Brown turned his focus to Bob's new last name. "Smailey! That's a good last name. I am sure it has served you well. Mr. Bob Smelly. Or is it Smiley?"

Bob laughed. He was used to this kind of hurtful treatment.

After some orientation, they put Bob to work. Their project was due in 17 days. They were analyzing the effects of five different metal densities on engine harnesses.

As Bob started his introductory assignment on his computer, Beatrice Jones came over to him. She leaned in and put both hands on his desk. "Just so you know, everything you produce we are going to go over with a fine-tooth comb. You think you are hot stuff, Mr. Summa Cum Laude. Well, you're about to enter the real world."

He smiled. Bob knew that Beatrice was amazing, but like Gary and Baxter, she had her problems.

Bob had worked for another firm until he reached his mandated retirement age. Then he joined this firm, which was happy to hire him. Everything was at a slower pace here, and he had more time to get to know his coworkers. He knew these three people better than anyone else. He had worked with them for the last eight years, right up until his death.

Before Bob left this earth, he wanted to see what had made them so petty. Each member of the team was brilliant, but they behaved like children. He had learned to let their insults roll off him like water. Yet, he wondered why they were so unkind and, at the same time, caring. These three people were the only ones who had come to his funeral.

Bob had died alone, bald, and old, but now he was in his 20's and had hair past his shoulders.

Almost every day for eight years, his boss Gary had said some comment about his being bald. They still echoed in Bob's head, "Boy, that's shiny...smoother than a baby's bottom...the cone head is in the building."

Gary was always commenting on people's hair, and never

once, that Bob could remember, was the comment complimentary.

Walking into Gary's office, Bob was about to find out what was going on in his boss' mind. Without Gary realizing it, Bob stepped into Gary, entering him at will. Bob did a ghost merge.

Bob was inside Gary. He made his way into Gary's brain. It was overwhelming—all the thoughts, the insecurities, the pressures, the hopes, the love of his children, his wife, his staff. Bob searched for the thought train that contained "hair." It didn't take long. He dug into the memory bank. There were thousands of memories here.

Bob was amazed at the variety of ways Gary had insulted people over the years. "Did you get caught in a wind storm? Has a cuckoo bird nested on your head?"

Deeper and deeper, Bob sorted through the memories. He was looking for the first memory, the oldest entry in the file. And there it was, fully intact.

Little Gary is sitting on the kitchen chair, a towel over his shoulders, his mom cutting his hair. The phone rings. She picks it up. She keeps cutting Gary's hair, but she isn't paying close attention. She finishes the call and takes off the towel.

She looks at Gary and laughs. The haircut is uneven. He looks so funny. She laughs and laughs. Father gets home. He laughs. Brother laughs. The neighbors laugh. Everyone laughs at Gary.

Forty-six years later, Gary insults people daily about their hair.

Bob stepped out of Gary's skin. He looked at Gary. "It is good to be working here. Thanks for hiring me."

"OK, longhair, just get back to work." Gary paused, looking at him, "But Bob, know that my door is always open."

That phrase, "the door is always open" reminded Bob of his former house. He had accumulated so much stuff that he couldn't shut any of the interior doors, and he couldn't open the backdoor because it was blocked with books and packages. He smiled. He could name every book in the pile against the backdoor. Bob walked to his desk and sat down. He looked over to Baxter.

Baxter had a way of making fun of people that wasn't fun for anybody but Baxter. He noticed Bob looking at him. "Yeah, you can look at me all you want, but that doesn't mean you are going to get any smarter."

Bob got up and walked toward Baxter. "Where are you going, smart ass?"

Bob ignored the comment and walked behind Baxter and jumped into him. His feet entered at Baxter's shoulders. Plop. He went all the way in.

Wow, Baxter's mind was traveling full speed. He was analyzing everything he saw.

Bob was searching for insults. There was a huge jumble of them. The memory stream was loaded. "Hey dumb ass, you sit on your brains…Hey Pinocchio, it looks like you haven't told the truth in a long, long time…You sure do smell good when you eat onions."

Where did it all start? What was the root memory? Bob was going through chronologically, and there it was.

Baxter is a sophomore in high school. No one ever pays attention to him. He is smart and funny, but no one ever notices.

One of the cool kids is picking on a student who has dropped his cafeteria tray. The cool kid is pointing a finger at him and laughing. Lots of others are joining in pointing their fingers and laughing.

Baxter notices the kid has dropped his tray with chicken fingers on it. Baxter shouts out, "Let's give him more than a chicken finger. Let's give him a hand." Baxter starts clapping and the whole cafeteria joins in.

From that day forward, Baxter's pattern was set. All of his insults followed from that one moment.

Bob pulled out. He had seen enough. He was glad to get out of Baxter's head.

"Get back to your desk, rookie. You're benched," said Baxter.

A few minutes later, when Beatrice walked by, Bob hitched a ride. She was headed to pour a cup of coffee for herself. By the time she picked up the cup, Bob was part of her.

Bob explored her mind.

He was looking for why it was that Beatrice never complimented anyone's work but her own. He quickly saw that she had a huge file of memories admiring other people's work, but it always led to disdain.

Bob looked deeper. He tracked her neural pathways until he came to the crossroads, the very first intersection of trouble.

It is the last day of school in fourth grade. She is one of the people who have brought in the extra credit science report. She is proud of her work. The teacher has promised that the three best reports will be up on the corkboard after recess.

She is sure hers will be among them. She can't wait for recess to be over.

Beatrice races into the classroom, but her report isn't on the board. She can't believe it. She starts to cry. Her teacher asks her what is wrong. She says, "I wanted my report to be one of the best."

"I don't recall getting a report from you."

Beatrice thinks that means that the report was so unmemorable her teacher had already forgotten it. Beatrice goes back to her seat without a word.

Bob traveled through her unconscious memories to the moment that Beatrice had turned in the report. She lays it on her teacher's desk. There is a fan in the room blowing on the desk. The report slips off the desk and falls into the trashcan.

She had buried the whole disappointment in the back of her brain. But everyday of her life since then, she can't stand for other people to get recognition.

Bob released Beatrice and was now standing in the break room. She finished pouring her coffee and was startled to see Bob. She smiled, though, and said, "The coffee's always hot, and we keep creamer in the fridge."

Sitting at his desk, Bob wondered what he would find if

he went into his own mind. Why was he in this office? Why did he come back here?

He had no one in his life. His wife had divorced him 45 years ago. He had no children. No parents. No cousins. No room to walk in his house. All he had was his work and this team of injured individuals.

He liked them.

He would miss them.

He knocked on the opened door of Garry's office. "I don't think this is a good fit for me."

An hour later, Beatrice, Gary, and Baxter were shaking his hand goodbye.

"I told you it wouldn't be as easy as college," Beatrice said.

"Get a haircut, and maybe you'll get a new perspective," Gary added.

"Two thumbs up for the guy who is ready to do some serious thumb twiddling," Baxter said.

Bob walked out the door and lost his youthful appearance on the sidewalk. His long hair slipped onto the grass and disappeared like snow on a warm day. Bob felt the pain of his teammates, their brilliance, and their insecurity.

He knew they needed someone to understand them. "Or was it," Bob wondered, "that they needed to understand themselves?" Either way, it was time for Bob to leave. He was ready to face his own truths. The old bald man stepped into his future and disappeared into the afternoon sun.

Dead of Winter

Pablo pushed the horizontal handle on the gray door as quietly as he could. He had been crouching behind a table in the back of the warehouse. Wearing black coats and belts with handcuffs and guns, ICE agents were rounding up the other undocumented workers. They had Tomas, Mateo, and Esperanza. Pablo knew he would be next.

He slipped out the back door with barely a sound. An ICE agent was watching the back of the building, but a huge cluster of overgrown bushes obscured this particular door.

It was bitter cold, and 4" of snow had fallen last night. The snow had not made it to the ground under the cover of the evergreens. Pablo heard a voice and saw the agent on the other side of the bushes. Pablo carefully made his way to the far side of the heating exhaust vent. Steam poured out. The warmth of it was some comfort for Pablo, but this was clearly another bad day in his 33 years of existence.

About five minutes later, the door opened. An agent popped his head out, took a quick look around, called to the agent on the other side of the bushes, and went back inside. Pablo spied the other agent walking around the corner of the building toward the parking lot.

Pablo was pressed up against the brick building, the steam making his body hard to see. He was holding his breath, his bald head against the bricks.

He had taken to shaving his head because so much of his hair had fallen out. Three years of constant agony can do that.

Now he had to get away. On the other side of the bushes was a lawn and, beyond that, a woods. If he could just get across the snow-covered field and into the woods, he could make his way to the side road. From there, he could crisscross his way the two miles to his apartment.

He crawled through the bushes to the edge of the lawn. There was no one in sight. Pablo took off running, like he had in his youth when a soccer ball had been kicked in front of him, and he was racing for the winning goal. The lawn was only 100 yards to the woods, but the snow and ice slowed him down, and it was hard to run in boots.

Pablo didn't stop as he entered the woods. He ran for about two minutes, gradually going slower and slower. He kept his hands in his jean pockets, then alternated them for warmth by cupping his hands over his nose, then his ears, then jamming his hands back into his pockets. He finally stopped to catch his breath. Leaning against a huge oak tree, he pulled his shirt up to his head to try to lessen the cold.

The temperature was 11° F. His coat was back in the warehouse locker room. His breath billowed as it rose up through his shirt into the late afternoon air.

As he stood under the shelter of the tree, he heard a familiar voice. "You got this, bro. You'll be home before you know it. Keep going."

The voice was from his younger brother, Juan. Together, they had escaped the gangs in Honduras, traveled through Guatemala and into Mexico, and eventually the United States. In the desert, Juan had died from dehydration.

Ever since, Pablo would hear his brother's voice, especially in times of trouble.

Pablo started walking again. There was a deep ravine. He headed down the steep slope. He lost his footing and slipped onto his back. He slid in the snow, rolled over a stump, and finally came to a stop as he crashed into a fallen tree.

He lay there in the snow for a moment, groaning. He thought of his daughters, Sofia and Mariana. They were 3 and 4 years old. He thought of how they had never seen snow and a happy image came to him of their black hair flying up in the breeze as they slid through the snow. He had never held Sofia and hadn't seen Mariana in three years. Every week, he called Isabella, his wife, and talked to the kids. Every month, he sent them money.

Every month he did this was another month he and his family survived. The gang members had told him they would kill him if he didn't pay for their protection. How could he pay money he didn't have? Pablo tried the only thing he could think of, which was to come to the United States. He knew he wasn't wanted there. He felt like a hunted criminal, but he managed to earn the money to keep his family alive.

"Get up. You can't lie in the snow. "

"Yeah," Pablo said out loud. He righted himself and slowly stood up, pushing his hands into his pockets. His fingers were burning. His ears were white from frostbite. His back had snow clinging to it from the fall.

Pablo was now at the bottom of the ravine. He thought he was getting close to the road. There was a frozen stream he needed to cross. His foot went through the ice. When he tried to pull it out, his boot got caught and then his other foot went through.

The water wasn't deep, but it was higher than his boots. He managed to get out after a couple of seconds. He had to take off his boots to pour out the water. One of his socks came off. He rung out the water and went to put his sock back on. His foot was stuck to the ice, just enough so he needed to peel it off with his hands.

Now he was up, across the creek, heading toward the road. He didn't actually know where the road was. He had never been in these woods, but he was fairly sure he was headed in the right direction.

"You're doing good, man! Keep it up. Don't stop walking."

Pablo said, "Juan, I can't feel my fingers."

"Keep going, bro. You got this."

Pablo stopped. He saw a thicket of bushes. It had a spot where he could see a pile of leaves that didn't have snow on them. He walked over to it. His feet were heavy. They felt like ice blocks.

"You can't stop. Keep walking, man. You are close to the road."

Falling to his knees, Pablo got under the bushes. He tried to cover himself with leaves, but they were in frozen clumps that wouldn't come off the ground. Lying there shivering, he closed his eyes.

"No, you don't. Come on. It's time to go."

Pablo heard the voice so clearly that it felt real, like his brother was with him again. He opened his eyes.

Now he could see his brother wearing his short sleeve shirt, but it was clean, not like the day Pablo had buried him in it. Juan reached out and put his hand on Pablo's cheek. His hand was warm and comforting, like the desert just after sunset.

Juan said, "I got you, bro. You're going to be fine. I'll sit with you awhile so that you can rest."

Pablo saw his brother sit down. He felt his own head being lifted, and now, he was resting in the lap of his brother. Pablo could feel some warmth, like his brother was cupping his hands over his ears.

Staring ahead at the thicket of bushes, Pablo noticed his breath misting in the twilight. He saw the leaves on the ground glistening with frost. He became very still. His breathing slowed.

In this moment, under the bushes with his head in the lap of his dead brother, Pablo took his last breath. His final hope was that he would become a comforting voice for Isabella, Mariana, and Sofia.

Hot Seat

Jack Johnson strolled into his new office. It was a corner office. The recent past was a blur for him, but now, after the accident, he had been promoted to the job he deserved.

He ran his hand through his short, grey hair and looked around at the high ceilings, the beautiful large windows, the mahogany desk, and a high-back leather chair. Somehow, he had made it.

He remembered feeling like his life was falling apart. Everything seemed to be catching up to him, like that long string of unanswered emails, the never-returned phone calls, his fits of rage, and his supposed lack of regard for other people's feelings.

Then there was also a memory of driving to an appointment and hitting a patch of ice, losing control of his car, and hitting a pillar in the overpass.

Now he had a new job and a corner office. It was funny how life had a way of correcting itself.

His secretary was named Pele. Standing next to her desk, Jack asked her, "What kind of name is that?"

"It's one my parents liked," she said.

"No, I mean, what ethnic background is it?"

"Oh, I know what you mean."

"Well, what is it?"

"It is just what you think."

"I didn't say what I think."

"Good, then everything is settled." Pele began to work on some papers scattered on her desk.

Jack went back to his cushy office. He wasn't going to let that woman get on his nerves.

He checked the phone and had two voice messages. The first one was a request for help and advice. Jack said out loud, "It will be a cold day in hell before I help her out."

The second call was a request for him to attend a meeting next week. He thought, "Don't they know I have a secretary? I am not going to waste my time answering that call."

His phone vibrated. A text from Ralph Green read, "Please call me."

Jack thought that Ralph hadn't heard the news about his promotion. Ralph was once his boss, but he couldn't order him around anymore. If Ralph wanted to talk, he would have to be the one to make the call. Jack pounded a fist on his desk. "Why doesn't Ralph just leave me alone?"

There were 23 emails that Jack opened. Everyone wanted something, but nothing that he cared about. No response was necessary.

Jack could use a coffee, though. He got on the intercom. "Pele, I would like a cup of coffee."

"That sounds good, sir."

"Yes, it does, and can I get cream and sugar in it?"

"I don't see why not."

Jack felt important as he sat at his desk in his new chair. He began to slide open each of his desk drawers. The lower left drawer would not open. "What the hell is going on here?" He picked up his phone. He would have the situation addressed immediately.

"Hello, maintenance, this is Jack Johnson in the 6th floor corner office. I have a desk drawer that I can't get open."

"All the drawers should open, sir."

"Yeah, well they don't all open. It's very frustrating having a new desk with a drawer that won't open. Can you get someone up here to fix it?"

"Yes, we can."

"Thank you, and don't keep me waiting."

"Not a problem, sir. We appreciate you. We know that you have done a lot to get where you are. We wish you the best of luck in your new position. It can't be easy being in the hot seat."

"Please, just do your job. I've got things to do."

Jack got off the phone. It was a great feeling to have people working for him. The past 10 years had been a rat race. He had often felt that he had to hide from trouble. Everyone wanted a piece of him. No more. Now he was in control. He didn't have to answer to anybody.

Where was that coffee, though? "Pele, where is my coffee?"

"I don't know. I haven't seen it."

"You didn't bring it to me like I asked."

"Oh, did you ask me to bring you a cup of coffee? I'm sorry. I must have missed that."

"Missed it?" Jack shouted. "You miss it again and it will be the last day you work for me. Get me a coffee and be quick about it."

"I hear you loud and clear."

"Don't make me ask again."

Jack had a couple new emails come in. He said to himself, "Everybody wants to know what I think. Can't they think for themselves?" He decided he didn't need to respond.

He walked over to the big window. It was hot in the office. Next to the big window was a smaller, double-hung window. Jack tried to open it, but it wouldn't budge. "You've got to be kidding me," he growled.

Where was his coffee? He probably should have made it an iced coffee. He walked out of the office. "Pele, did you get my coffee yet?"

"No, Jack."

"Make it an iced coffee. My office is quite warm, and I didn't see a thermostat. Do you know where it is?"

"Yes, I do."

Jack waited a couple of seconds for her to continue, but she didn't. "Where is it?"

"It's not in your office."

"I know that."

"Then why did you ask?"

"I didn't ask that. Don't be a smart ass."

"Good, well I am off to the coffee shop." Pele got up abruptly and walked away from Jack.

He went back in the office and closed the door. That woman wouldn't be working for him much longer. Man it was hot. He sat back down in his chair. He tried the stuck drawer once again. It didn't open so he called maintenance again.

"Hey, Einstein, I would really like to get my desk fixed."

"Is there anything else you would like fixed, sir?"

"No, I just want the desk drawer to open. No, wait, the window is also stuck. Get somebody up here to fix it now. Is that clear?"

"That must be frustrating, a nice new office and the door won't open. You're stuck inside."

"The door is fine. It's the window and the drawer that won't open."

"I know a guy with your experience is going to be in that office for the long haul. Let us know if there is ever anything we can do for you." The phone clicked, but it didn't go dead. Jack heard, "Yeah, it was him again. He hasn't figured it out yet." Jack heard a burst of laughter. Then the phone did go dead.

Jack was sweating. He wasn't wearing a coat, but he unbuttoned his shirt a bit. He tried the window again. No luck.

He was having some trouble breathing. He went to the door and put his hand on the knob. "Ouch." The doorknob was hot, like it was on fire.

He called out, "Pele, are you there?"

"Yes, I am here."

"I can't open the door. The knob is hot."

"Oh my, that can't be good. What did you do?"

"I didn't do anything. Please open the door."

"I can't do that. You have already said the knob is hot."

"Use a towel or a handkerchief to get it open."

"That is not possible. I am on my coffee break. I shouldn't even be talking to you."

"Shut your trap, and open the door!" There was silence on the other side.

Jack began to scream. "I said open the door. Open the damn door, or you're fired. Open it right now."

Jack listened. There was laughter.

He pounded on the door. "I'm not kidding. Open the door, or you'll be fired."

"No, Mr. Johnson, you can't fire me. I don't work for you. I am above your pay grade. But there is someone who is being fired right now. Can you guess who it is?"

"Don't joke with me. Open this damn door." Jack's hands stung as he hit the door. The door was blistering hot. The whole office was hot. He walked back over to his chair and sat down to think.

The chair was hot, too. It was burning him. He tried to get up, but he was stuck to the seat.

There in the corner office, Jack received the rewards for all the things he had done and hadn't done. His new career was red hot and so was his seat.

Warmth

Twenty-nine-year-old salesman Henry Gibbons was looking out the backdoor, staring at the woods. He was feeling compelled to tell a ghost story. He wasn't sure what the story would be, but he found himself searching for his boss, the hostess of the party.

The party was designed to bring the families of the employees together for a mid-summer celebration. It was at the CEO's house, which was ablaze with lights and people.

Henry spotted her. "Cleo," he said, "I was thinking that it would be fun for the children if I told them a story. I love kids, and you know I always have something to say."

"That would be lovely," Cleo said. "Perhaps you could calm them down. I will gather them on the deck."

"Perfect." Henry said, as he thought, "I will give them a bit of a fright."

He thought the woods should be part of the story because they were nearby and mysterious. He felt it really didn't matter what he said. It was all make believe. The important thing was to get the kids to listen and give them a good scare.

When the children were seated, Henry had them turn and look at the woods. The grass behind the deck stretched for about 150 feet. Then there was a split-rail, cedar fence and another stretch of grass, maybe 20 feet or so. And then the woods started, thick and dark.

"What do you suppose is in those woods?" asked Henry.

"There is a raccoon that lives in there," said one of the boys.

"That is right," said Henry. "And did you know that there are also creatures in the woods that aren't alive?"

The children puzzled at this question.

"Yes, these creatures are a shadow of their former selves. They are men and women, just like the adults at this party, but they have been captured and turned to shadows."

Henry took a drink of his beer and looked at the children. Their eyes were wide. He had their full attention.

"When the sun sets, no one can see the shadows. That's when the shadow creatures come out of the woods and try to get warm. Since they are shadows, they are always cold, even on warm summer nights."

"How do they get warm?" asked Tony, one of the older kids. He was eight years old.

"They come into the houses of people like you and me."

Henry sipped his beer. The kids looked worried.

"Sometimes at night you might hear a whistling noise. It might be the wind, or it could be the shadow people trying to get into your house. They sound like this." Henry breathed in and out, making his breath whistle.

"And if they do get into your house, they will look for blankets. They will creep under them. If you happen to be under a blanket, the shadow people will nibble at your feet and ankles, or perhaps even your neck or tummy, trying to eat your warmth and make you one of them."

At that point, one of the little girls burst into tears. "I don't like this story."

The other children joined her, "This is too scary." Suddenly, almost all the children were crying.

Tony, the 8-year-old, said, "You are a bad man to make children cry."

The kids raced off the deck crying for their parents.

Henry shouted at them, "Calm down! It's just a funny story." A couple of minutes later, his boss appeared in the doorway. "What were you thinking? How could you tell such a story to the little ones?"

"Everybody likes a scary story," said Henry.

"Not like the one you told."

"I won't tell anymore tonight."

"Henry, I need you to leave. The children can't even look at you without crying. You should have known better."

Henry got his coat, said a couple of goodbyes, and high-fived one of his friends near the front door.

"Dude," said Henry's friend, "you're the one who makes the kids cry!"

Henry fired up his vintage Mustang, did a quick U-turn, and then took a left on Woods Drive. The sun had just set.

When Henry was about a mile into the forest, his car shuddered. Ten seconds later, it died.

After a few times trying to start the car, he got out and shut the door so no mosquitoes, moths, or whatever else was flying in the twilight would get into his car.

Henry pulled up the hood and stared at the engine compartment. He could hardly see anything. He went back to open up the car and grab his phone. It was locked. The keys and his phone were inside. It was one of the dilemmas of having a vintage car. It was easy to lock the door with your keys inside.

He went back to the front of the car and closed the hood.

At that instant, Henry felt something on his neck. He thought maybe it was a bug and slapped his neck to try to kill it. Whatever it was, he felt a definite sting.

He shrugged it off and started walking back toward the party. A few steps into the trip, he saw a shadow move across the road in front of him. The woods were dense on each side of the road. Henry thought that it must have been the last bit of light mixing with the coming night. Yet, he suddenly felt uncomfortably alone.

A few steps more and Henry saw another shadow pass in front of him. He stopped walking. He could hear the wind whistling through the trees.

A second later, he literally jumped in the air as he once again felt something on the back of his neck. It was more than a tingling. It was painful, like a bee sting. He couldn't find the bee.

He rubbed his neck. It was wet. Was it sweat or blood? He looked at his fingers. They had blood on them.

Henry decided to jog back to the party. He could hear his steps on the gravel crunching the rocks. Every step seemed loud. He wondered if he was calling attention to himself in the stillness. Perhaps he should walk quietly along this deserted road?

He felt another sting on his neck. This time lower, though, and more towards his back. That pain made him start to sprint. He was running to get out of those woods. At this pace, he would be out in just a few minutes.

He felt a bite on his ankle. Something was tearing into him. He screamed and tried to swat at his leg while running and tripped himself. He tumbled to the ground. His neck, his back, his right ankle felt like they were on fire. As he climbed to his knees, he heard a low whistle coming from above. He turned toward it and saw a shadow hovering over the ground. A kind of breathy whistle emanated from it.

Henry managed to get himself up. He forced himself to run. He could see the streetlamp for the neighborhood in the distance.

One foot, now the next, now the next.

He felt he was in slow motion. The shadow was at his side. Then the pain hit his neck. He grabbed at it and felt a jolt of pain in his fingertips. Then it jumped to his whole hand and arm. The pain was spreading across his body.

He would not stop running. One foot, now the next, now the next.

He looked at his fingers and saw that they were gone. All he could see of his hand was shadow. The pain moved from his neck to his face. He stopped running.

Henry collapsed from a stabbing pain in his legs. He looked at himself and saw nothing but shadow.

He felt himself being lifted off the ground. The woods, the woods, he was moving into the woods. He lost consciousness.

After a bit, he awoke. His sight was unclear, as if he was looking through a veil. He raised his hand and saw a shadowy outline. Then he raised his other hand. Nothing but shadow. He was shivering from the cold. He found himself wandering through the woods. Wherever he looked, he went. He glided through the dense growth.

He looked up and traveled upward to the tops of the trees. He looked down and slid downward. Something caught his attention, and he went towards it.

Henry came to the edge of the woods. He saw a stretch of grass, and a cedar fence, and a house ablaze in light.

Playing, laughing on the deck were children.

"Warmth," said Henry very slowly. He took a deep, whistling breath.

Right Here

What do you do when you can't keep up with your work? That's the question I asked her, even though she was dead at the time.

No one says it is easy being a front line worker at Job and Family Services. Even for the people who don't seem to care, it's a hard job.

My problem is that I am one of the people who care too much. There are certain individuals who come into this office who are desperate. After you have been through a thousand people or so, you start to recognize who is truly desperate.

When I spot them, I make sure I do everything I can for them. That takes time.

That's the problem. That extra time isn't in my job description. I have a quota of people I need to get through, or at least I did.

One day, I was in the break room by myself feeling over-whelmed. My numbers were low. My job was at risk. I looked at the picture hanging on the wall by the vending machine. It was of Miss Mable Ann Rutherford, who had been the employee of the year six times.

Staring at her picture, wishing that she was still alive and could talk with me, I asked silently, "How do I do it? How do I help these people and keep up with my job?"

I shut my eyes for a few seconds. I heard the clock tick-ing. Then I thought someone was in the room with me. I opened my eyes and saw a cloudy figure standing by the vending ma-chine. It looked like Miss Mable Ann. She seemed to answer me clear as day, "You do what you can."

I said out loud, "What do you mean?"

She leaned toward me. "Oh, dear Shaneeka, I mean to say that every person needs something different. You have to pay attention to see how you might help. There isn't a rule. You just do what you can."

I could see her clearly now. I told her, "I don't know what to do. And everything I do takes time. That's time I don't have. I am always behind."

"Sometimes you touch a person's hand to reassure them. Sometimes you look them in the eye for an extra second or two so that they know that you really see them." She stopped talking for a moment and smiled at me. She sent her reassuring gaze to me. She shrugged her shoulders and added, "Sometimes you give them a phone number that you handwrite, even though you've got a preprinted sheet with the number already on it. That way, they know it's for them."

Her eyes locked on mine. "You just do what you can."

"Thank you, Miss Mable."

"No, thank you, Shaneeka, for caring."

After that, I felt Miss Mable was always with me. If I had a question, I checked in with Miss Mable. I couldn't see her, but I felt her presence and heard her voice.

Once, someone came to my station and I felt they weren't telling the truth. I silently asked, "What do you think of this person, Miss Mable?"

"As slithery as a snake."

Another time, I looked out at my line, and I saw Miss Mable with her arm around a lady. She was holding that woman up. When that woman, Mrs. Rodriguez, came up to me and shared her story, I spent extra time with her and made sure all of her paperwork was complete.

I know my boss means well. She does care about people. But she told me that I am deficient. Other people have to pick up my slack.

I see how they do it. They call it "burning through." It is the way to keep from being fired. Ironic isn't it. You race through your cases, "burn through" those cases, so that your contact numbers are good.

When you do that, you can't think about each person. You can't take time to hold their hand or make a special phone call for them. You have one goal: Process them as quickly as possible.

I did improve my numbers but not enough. Then today happened.

Sheila Gunderson came through my line with her little boy, Bradley, at her side. She was wearing sunglasses on a cloudy day. Her hands were trembling.

She needed immediate assistance. We have a program for what she needed, but she was in the wrong line. She waited 30 minutes with her son in the wrong line.

It wasn't my job to help her. It wasn't my job to get her in the right line. It was my job to get rid of her as quickly as possible.

But I didn't do my job.

I talked to her. I put my hand on hers. I smiled at her. I picked up her boy. I saw behind her glasses. I saw the swelling and the purple skin. I took her to the right line.

But she couldn't wait. She said her husband would already be furious. I saw her go out the back door to the parking lot.

My boss saw the whole exchange. She was waiting for me when I got back to my desk. She was upset that I had left my station. She fired me. My numbers are her numbers.

Things got really crazy just after that. Sheila's husband pulled his car over before they even left the parking lot. He pulled out a gun. He shot his wife. He shot his son. Then, he shot himself.

So here I am cleaning out my desk. The agency doors are locked for the night. And Sheila is standing with her little boy, right here.

She is standing right here next to my desk, looking at me without the sunglasses, but with agony in her eyes and her boy at her side in a daze. She tells me she doesn't know where else to go.

I try to give her a hug, but, of course, I can't.

I can't pick up the boy to hold him on my lap, to whisper to him that it's all over now, that everything is going to get better.

I call, "Miss Mable, Miss Mable, Miss Mable. I need your help. I know you know where Sheila and Bradley need to go. You can help them, can't you?"

Miss Mable appears from the dark of the closed office. She gives Sheila a hug. She smiles at Bradley and takes his hand.

They are headed up the stairs now. Miss Mable has her arm around Sheila. They are going up the grand staircase. It is filled with light. They stop and turn towards me.

Sheila says, "Thanks for trying to help."

Bradley waves bye-bye.

Alone now, I gather my things and head down the stone stairs without a job. I don't know what I am going to do, but I know I am going to do what I can.

Stage Fright

John Zoowolski waited backstage trying not to sweat. He heard a creaking noise behind him. He turned around to see a door opening.

A short man appeared in the doorway. The glow of a red light filled the room behind him. He stared at John. "Nervous?" he asked.

John nodded. His stomach was on a rollercoaster ride.

"You got a big presentation coming up, don't you?"

"Yes," John's voice quivered as he spoke.

"And you're worried it's not going to go well. I can see it on your face."

John tried to keep from shaking, but his right leg began to bounce ever so slightly. This man wasn't helping things.

"Want to see something that you will never forget?" the man asked ominously.

John managed to get enough breath to say, "No thanks, I am trying to concentrate." He took a couple of steps away from the man.

"Oh, you don't want to miss this!" The man lurched forward and grabbed John by the wrist. His grip was like a vice, and he pulled John into the red room. John wanted to scream but didn't want to make a scene while the program was happening on stage.

The red room was a closet filled with cables and microphone stands. John tried to push his way out, but the little man was like a solid wall. The door creaked shut. The man stared into John's eyes. "My name is Nick, and you're going to need to shut your eyes." The red light went out.

"What do you see?" asked Nick.

"I don't see anything. It's pitch black in here."

"Close your eyes, and you'll see something."

John blinked and saw a flash of light. He blinked again and saw more light. He shut his eyes and instantly saw himself on the stage. The bright lights were shining in his face. Sweat was glistening on his forehead. "I seem to have forgotten what I was going to say." Laughter rippled through the theater.

Opening his eyes, John couldn't see anything. Blindly he walked towards the door, but he couldn't find it. The man seemed to be gone. The room seemed to have no walls. John stopped moving.

The voice of Nick came out of the darkness, "Shut your eyes. What do you see now?"

More out of fear than obedience, John shut his eyes. He saw himself pointing to a slide on the screen. Then he saw the audience. One person yawned. Another person nodded off. The theater filled with the sound of snoring.

John opened his eyes and quivered, "Let me out of here."

"No, first I want to show you something really scary. Shut your eyes again."

"I am not shutting them."

Nick said, "You have given away your choice. Fear controls you."

John's eyes closed. He saw the conference center from outside. In the afternoon sky, a fiery meteor came thundering down. It crashed into the complex. John saw inside the theater at the moment of impact. Death was everywhere.

Nick screamed, "Choose."

John stood paralyzed, scared to death.

"Choose now."

"What choice do I have?"

"The choice is between fear or triumph. Close your eyes, and imagine what you want to have happen."

The door creaked open. The red light came on. John was standing alone in the closet. He stepped out. He wiped off his forehead and staggered over to the side curtain. John saw the VP of tech support going through her final slides. He would be next.

He looked at the backstage wall. There was a photo with the caption, "In memory of Nick Garland, stage manager for 16 years." John read on, "Prepare for your moment, and choose your destiny today."

John caught his breath. He put his thumb under his chin and his index finger on his cheek. He slowly reread the statement. He studied the man in the photo. He muttered under his breath, "Choose."

John took a deep breath. He shut his eyes and imagined himself on the stage—the way he wanted to be.

Undecided

Abe Demsky's career had skyrocketed. In eight years, she had gone from a sales rep to a shift manager to a unit manager to a division manager to a regional vice president.

She had a way with words, a way with people, and a dead man sitting next to her in her car.

Her full name was Colleen Abraham Demsky. She was almost six feet tall and had curly black hair. She was named after her grandmother Colleen on her mother's side and her grandfather Abraham on her father's side. When she was a baby, her father had started calling her Abe, and the name stuck.

Abe was on her way to a high-level meeting at her corporate office of Every Which Way Wireless, one of the largest telecom companies in existence. Her boss, the CEO of the company, Lionel Perkins, had called the meeting. Abe had flown in the night before, stayed at a hotel, and was now in the limo traveling to the meeting.

The dead man sitting next to her had shown up in her condo three days earlier, the same day she got the word about the special meeting of top execs.

When she first saw him, it was 1 a.m. and she had just closed her laptop. She was about to go brush her teeth.

There he was sitting in her grandmother's chair in the living room. He was looking out the window. She gasped and let out a muffled scream, her hand over her mouth.

She would have been more alarmed, but he was old and seemingly harmless.

He did not turn his head as she stepped toward him. "How did you get in here?"

He didn't move.

"Excuse me, sir. I am going to need you to leave. I don't know how you got in here, but it's time to go."

He tilted his head. He was listening.

Something was off, though. He wasn't breathing.

"Sir, are you all right? How did you get in here? Are you lost?"

No answer. No eye movement. No movement of his stomach or chest.

She bent down and touched his hand. Her hand went through his and touched the arm of the chair. She reeled back and stood looking at him and then her own fingers.

She wondered, "Did that really happen?" Her heart began to pound. The man was clearly here.

In amazement, she placed her hand on his head and pushed it into him. There was a slight resistance. Her hand was inside his head. All she felt was warmth. It was like she had put her hand in a warm oven. She was in the cold, and inside him was the warmth.

She pulled her hand out and looked at it, then him.

She couldn't think straight. She started to pick up her

phone but stopped. She was hallucinating. He couldn't really be here. She needed to go to bed.

She washed her hands for nearly two minutes. Lying in bed, she could see him standing in the darkness. He was in her room. She turned toward the wall next to her bed. In the morning, she would feel better.

She did not see him that next morning. After work, she was in her kitchen, and he walked in. She closed her eyes.

"My name was Clarence Waterbridge." His voice was soft and clear. "You have never seen me, but you have talked with me. You were the helpful young lady that brought my wife and me into the cell-phone era."

He looked at her. Her eyes were wide open. She was standing at the kitchen island. She began to break apart the lettuce for her salad.

His voice quivered. "You don't know me, but I know all about you. I have been watching you, listening to you, traveling with you."

Abe continued fixing her dinner. She thought she was losing it. Losing it. Losing it. It wasn't happening. This was the stressful price of too many 12 to 14 hour workdays.

"I am here to help my wife. I believe you are the one who is going to do it, the one who is not only going to make things right for my dear Ada but for 123,537 other people, as well."

Abe sliced the chicken. Losing it.

"Your meeting." He nodded his head and raised his hand. "That's when you are going to have the fight of your life." He walked out of the kitchen and sat back in the living room chair.

She ate dinner and tried to let go of what she had just heard. Abe got onto her computer. Nineteen emails later, she went to bed. He watched her trying to sleep. He knew that she could set things right. His sweet Ada shouldn't have to suffer like this.

On the plane ride to Atlanta, he was there standing in the aisle, unaffected by turbulence.

In the hotel room, he sat in the recliner. He did not speak.

She ignored him and focused on the business at hand, a never-ending stream of communication with her people. She had to hold a lot of hands to keep it all going, to keep the numbers climbing.

Now in the limo, Clarence turned to Abe. In his precise voice, he said, "You told me when you signed us up for our wireless plan that everything would be easy. There was no risk because we could always talk with the helpful people at your company."

Abe glanced towards him.

"You even called me up after my first bill had come and made sure I understood the charges. I was so happy with you and your extra effort to make sure that we were satisfied that I gave you the names and phone numbers of friends who also might want to work with such nice people."

He gave a short laugh. "I now know you were not being totally honest with me. I see how your company works. You are not the nice people I thought you were, but I know that you are not all bad either. It is time to make things right."

The meeting included 12 people. It would be over long before lunch because lunch would be at the club, and the afternoon agenda would be golf.

There was one empty chair in the boardroom. It was directly across from Abe, and the dead Mr. Waterbridge was sitting in it.

Lionel Perkins sat at the head of the table. He was 6 foot three inches, 260 pounds, Ivy League MBA. His laugh could be heard through the glass walls of the corporate meeting room.

They began on schedule. Abe brought her laser focus into the content of the material. Like the last 15 quarters, the numbers were up. Then came the announcement.

"We have decided," said Lionel, "that we are going to expand the period of positive engagement with undecided customers from six months to two years."

The CEO let that message settle in. "This will bring our termination rate down to a trickle."

Abe knew exactly what this meant. Her mind flashed ahead to countless issues that would arise, countless creative conversations she would have with her team. She looked across the table. Clarence Waterbridge was staring her down.

She was uncomfortable with his gaze but more so with what her boss had just said. Adrenaline poured into her system. She looked at her boss. Her courage came to her lips. "Do you think that is wise?"

Lionel smiled. He was a leader that didn't like discussion about decisions that had already been made. "Of course, it is wise. Like everything, it has pros and cons. But are we to focus on the negatives or move forward with the positives? We already know how much this policy has helped us. Let's leverage this situation to get the most out of it."

"Excuse me, Lionel, but may we address the elephant in the room?"

"No, we may not. There is no elephant. Some things remain unspoken. We know what needs to be done. We don't gather the best and the brightest to discuss every little detail."

Abe stood up and pushed back her chair. "Oh come on, Lionel. You know damn well that I am among the most loyal and hardworking, but this policy is going to pull our company down. How you can't see that is beyond me."

"Sit down, Abe, you're done here."

"No, I am not, Lionel. It is time to say what needs to be said. Everyone, including you, is thinking about it. People who choose to leave our service should be cancelled. They shouldn't be called 'undecided.' And it is not 'positive engagement' to keep billing them for services they have chosen to opt out of."

Lionel was silent for a moment and looked on in disbelief as Abe continued.

"Take the case of Mrs. Adeline Waterbridge. She has recently come to my attention. I looked up her details yesterday. Five months ago, she called to cancel service. She got disconnected. She called back and she got stuck in the call-in navigation. We keep records of this. She called back nine times over the next three months trying to cancel."

"That's enough." Lionel stood up.

"Yes, Lionel, it is enough, but please sit down and hear me out."

"No, you are the one who is going to sit down, or you are going to walk out of here and never return."

"Fine. Fire the VP of your hottest market. But before you do, I am going to speak my mind."

Abe turned her focus from Lionel to the other members in the room. The chair across from her was now empty.

Lionel let out a shout of protest but then went silent.

Abe continued, "Mrs. Waterbridge followed up her phone calls with two letters to cancel, but we kept billing her. We claimed to never have received the letters. That is not 'positive engagement.' And she is just one of 123,537 people who are being 'positively engaged.' They are on artificial respiration. That business is dead, but we keep billing them, and then we turn their unpaid bills over to collections. That is bad business, and it is going to kill us."

Abe sat down. She looked at Lionel.

Mr. Waterbridge was now standing next to Lionel and appeared to be whispering in his ear. Lionel was in his seat grimacing.

Mr. Waterbridge was actually biting Lionel's ear. He had his teeth locked onto that ear so that the big man couldn't move or speak.

Lunch was about to be delayed. The numbers for next quarter were going to decline by more than 6%, a huge loss in revenue. Heads were going to roll.

The next CEO of Every Which Way Wireless was going to be a woman who had an honest vision for growth and who was willing to stand up for the little guy that silently sits in the room.

But even the little guys have teeth.

The Dust

It was 6:50 a.m. Leslie put the key into the lock in the large oak door. She turned the key and pushed the handle. The hinges creaked open. She stood there in the doorway as light from the partially opened door streamed into the dark office space.

She saw something. It moved through the light towards the back of the office.

The bright morning sun was like a wedge of light in the office. Leslie had just seen something solid go through it. Of course, it could have been a shadow, maybe from a bird. A shadow up against the wall, yes, that was it. What else could it have been?

Leslie looked more closely at that beam of light in the dark office. Coming in and out of the light were a hundred specks of dust, or thousands, or was it millions? She watched the dance of the little particles swirling through the light. She noticed little tiny fibers, perhaps hair, and miniscule pieces of what? Earth, carpet, skin?

As the tiny particles floated in their airborne dance, Leslie was amazed how they totally disappeared in the shadows. The instant they were out of the wedge of light, they were gone.

They weren't really gone. They weren't visible though. She looked hard. She couldn't see them.

In the stream of light, though, there they were. Dancing.

How old were these particles of dust? Were they left over from the last time the office was vacuumed? Were they one week old, or a month, a year, a century? Who knew what was actually swirling through that room?

How could Leslie know what she was actually breathing? These tiny particles, hidden in the shadows were part of her, inside her each time she took a breath.

Leslie cleared her throat and turned on the lights. The dance disappeared.

She walked through the hall to the office area. This building was more than 100 years old. It had been sold numerous times. The original owner had gone bankrupt some 60 years ago. Leslie's company had been here for about a year. It was true this building had more space than their last building, but after the move, Leslie had noticed a new air of distrust. People didn't seem to get along as well as they once did.

Lately, this feeling had intensified. At her desk was another bright pink piece of paper, just like the others. This one had only one word: "Bitch."

She sat down on her chair, stretched out her arms, brought her fingers to the back of her head, and scratched.

Who was doing this?

The first paper she had received said: "Control Freak."

Then she had received another that said: "Up Tight."

Another said: "Know It All."

Her brain turned its gears. She ran through the people

in the office. Who was leaving her these messages? She had arrived early today, and she had been the last one to leave the office last night. Whoever was doing this was doing it long after office hours.

She hadn't told anyone else about this. That seemed risky. Since the move, people seemed more competitive than cooperative. Even though she worked with them everyday, she didn't trust her coworkers. A new common phrase around the office had become, "It's a dog eat dog world."

"Hi, Leslie." It was the owner of the company.

"Oh, good morning, Chuck. Nice to see you. I like that tie."

"You're in early, aren't you?"

"I woke up early and decided I might as well get started with payroll. The staff likes it when they get paid!"

"Thank you, Leslie. You're a hard worker. I appreciate all the time you give to our business." Chuck paused for a second. It looked like he wanted to say something important. He opened his mouth and stopped. "Well, let's have a good day." Chuck went into his office.

Leslie wondered, could it be Chuck? Of course, it could be. It could be anyone.

As the clock was chiming eight o'clock, the star salesman, Steve, strolled in. He said to Leslie, "What's up Raggedy Anne?"

"Not much Hulk. How you doing?"

"If I was doing any better, it wouldn't be legal."

Maybe it was Steve? He loved a good practical joke, but this didn't seem like a joke.

At 11:30, the office was abuzz with work. All 15 office employees and several of the traveling sales staff were in the office. A symphony of voices, keyboard taps, and the churning of the printer were the background sounds to Leslie's thoughts. A plan had hatched. Tonight she would find out who was leaving these stupid notes.

For dinner that night, she grilled a chicken breast, shredded it, and mixed it with assorted baby greens, pears, and blue cheese, then a few walnut halves. It was delicious with a bit of poppy seed dressing. She cleaned up and went back to the office.

It was nearly 8 p.m. when she arrived. The last rays of the sun were streaming through the west window. She didn't turn on the office lights. She saw the dust swirling, dancing through a slice of sunlit air.

Since she had parked her car a block away, no one would know she was here. This was her mission, and her mission alone. As she watched the tiny particles float through the air, Leslie finalized her plan. She would sit behind the workstation that housed the supply cabinet and printer. From there, she could see the whole office. She would catch the person who found the time to come in after hours and put a juvenile note on her desk. She would give him a piece of her mind.

The room grew dark. She felt a little chill. She looked over to where Margaret's desk had been. Margaret had died last month. She had a heart attack after arriving early at the office. Chuck found her. It was an uneasy feeling to be alone in the same room where someone had recently died.

Margaret wasn't the only one to die in this room. Leslie thought about the dreadful history of the building, how that original owner had refused to leave and was eventually shot dead by police, but not before he shot and killed two people, all in this same room.

Leslie tried to calm herself down and in the process grew sleepy. She sat on the floor and involuntarily closed her eyes. When she awoke, it was 2 a.m. Leslie got up and walked to her desk. No new paper, she let out a sigh of relief.

With her pen flashlight, she looked about the office. It was eerily quiet. An idea came to her. She walked towards Chuck's office. She shined the light on his desk. If she opened the desk drawers, would she find pieces of pink paper?

She opened one of the drawers. There were a stapler, glue sticks, and paper clips. She opened another drawer. It was filled with paper, all kinds, but no bright pink paper like the ones that had been left on her desk.

In the third drawer, she found a notebook. She flipped it open. There were random notes, something about vacation possibilities and building upgrades.

She went to put the notebook back but noticed an orange piece of paper. It said: "Bank Fraud." The clear printing was the same as her notes. Under that paper were two more: "Close Now" and "Death."

Leslie didn't know what to think. She put the pieces of paper and the notebook back in the drawer, shut it, and walked out of the office. It appeared someone was leaving notes for Chuck, as well. Why hadn't he said anything?

Leslie walked to the sales office. She went inside and over to Steve's desk. She carefully looked through the various drawers. In his top drawer, she found a couple of red papers with that same clear printing on them. "Liar." And the other saying: "Phony."

She returned to her spot behind the copier and sat back on the floor. She wasn't the only one getting the notes. Why hadn't anyone said anything to her? Why hadn't she checked with them? Had Margaret been getting the notes, too?

Leslie walked through the dark office over to the storage closet. She opened the door and saw Margaret's desk pushed against the unfinished wall. In the quiet of the closet, Leslie was overcome with sadness. She wasn't close to Margaret, but she had liked her. The image of the body bag being wheeled out of the office entered her mind. Poor Margaret.

Opening the drawers one by one, Leslie searched for a note. There it was, in the bottom drawer, three pieces of yellow paper with the all-too-familiar printing on them. "Stupid. Friendless. Incompetent."

Leslie gasped and then broke out in tears. No one should be treated like that. Margaret was a faithful person. She was always there to be relied upon.

Was everyone in the office getting these notes? Did no one trust the office staff enough to say something? What was going on here? It didn't used to be like this. Leslie wiped her nose and cheeks and returned to her hiding place. She sat down and thought, "I wish Margaret would have trusted me."

A minute later, she scratched her wrist. The hair on her arm was standing up. She could somehow feel that this was the moment. Someone was about to arrive.

Or could it be that someone was already here? Perhaps he was here watching her. Or he was hiding in the ceiling, looking through the ductwork, through a vent.

Perhaps somebody was dressed all in black and was standing right here in the office, and she couldn't see him. Leslie began to bite her lip trying to keep it from trembling.

Her attention went to a rustling sound on the shelf next to the copier. A stack of white paper rose into the air, and from under it, a piece of pink paper began to move.

It was now in the air, as if someone was carrying it.

Leslie stood up dumbfounded and walked toward the paper. She had to see. It couldn't actually be happening like this, could it? She must be imagining it. The paper was slowly moving through the air, but no one was holding it.

She shined her flashlight on her desk as the paper landed. No one was there. Just the dust, shining in the beam of the flashlight, but for an instant, Leslie thought she could make out the shape of a hand in those specks of dust. A marking pen was moving now. A word being formed.

Leslie looked on in horror. "Time is…"

The marker moved cleanly across the paper. "Up."

Leslie tried to catch her breath. In the stream of light, she saw a shadowy head being formed out of the dust, a skull with sunken eyes. An angry voice said, "This is my building. Kill or be killed."

The skull began to scream, its mouth wide open, its teeth shining in the light. Leslie fell backwards and cringed. She was paralyzed in fear. She lost her balance and slipped all the way to the ground, the light still in her hand.

The scream continued. The beam of light shined toward the skull, which was now cracking apart. It broke into a thousand tiny pieces and swirled into the invisible shadows. The scream echoed throughout the room and then stopped. Leslie saw the dust in the beam of light. That was the dust that Leslie breathed every day. Each day, the whole staff breathed it. Leslie choked. She grabbed her throat. She couldn't swallow, couldn't move. She took a stunted breath and lost consciousness.

In her hand, the flashlight burned steady, pointing toward the ceiling, and in the beam of light, the dust danced. Now a new face slowly appeared in the light. It was the gentle face of Margaret. Her hands came into focus. They stroked Leslie's head and pushed back her hair.

Leslie awoke and opened her eyes. She saw the face of Margaret smiling at her in the beam of light. Leslie could scarce believe what she was seeing. Her hand holding the flashlight slipped down. The dust became invisible and so did Margaret.

In that moment, lying on the floor of the office, Leslie felt something new, or was it something old? It was just a speck, a tiny fragment, but Leslie could clearly feel it. It was trust coming back into her life.

Gift Box

Nancy had saved the gift boxes until the office holiday party. Each of the six boxes was impeccably wrapped in sparkling paper.

The staff gathered in the conference room. When everyone had a coffee, tea, or eggnog, she distributed the presents to each person. "These are from Buzz. Don't open yours until I read the note from him."

It was an emotional moment since Buzz, the office manager for the last 12 years, had passed away last summer. His was a quick death—diagnosed in June, dead in August. Yet, he had enough time to put final plans in place, and this was one of them.

Nancy read the note out loud. "My dear friends—and I always did consider you friends before employees—I want to give you a little something of what you have given to me. When you open your box, please know that I appreciated everything you did for our team. My best wishes to each of you. Sincerely, Buzz."

"You may now open your boxes," Nancy added.

The boxes were all about the size of a fist. They could have held candy, or jewelry, or a small woodcarving, but they all had the same thing in them.

Zach was the first to get his open. He laughed out loud, smiled, and looked around the room as if to see his old boss laughing with him, as they had done on so many occasions.

Sherry opened the paper carefully, not tearing any part of it. She opened the small lid of the box and looked inside. Tears filled her eyes, and her mind was flooded with a thousand affirmations her boss had given her.

Diego ripped the paper apart and yanked the lid off. He held the box up to eye level, peering inside. He closed his eyes and mouthed the words "thank you" into the air. His mind raced with the implications of what it meant. Once again, he was brainstorming with his old boss.

Tony carefully opened his gift, looked inside, and put the box back on the boardroom table. He crossed his arms on his chest and muttered loud enough for everyone to hear, "You cheapskate."

Of course, Buzz was in the room, at least in spirit. He was full to the brim with joy as he watched the gifts being opened, even if he was shaking his head at Tony's comment.

Jasmine opened her gift, folded up the wrapping paper, looked inside, and thought for a moment. She took out a handful of throat lozenges from her jacket pocket and put them in the box. She remembered how Buzz had once said to her, "Everything and everyone has a place."

After everyone else had finished, Nancy tore off the paper and opened her box. She saw that it was empty, just like all the rest had been.

It brought a smile to her face. She remembered all the times her boss had said, "Every situation is what you make of it." He had wrapped each of these gifts with care. His personal touch was evident. She felt his reassuring presence in the empty box, and everywhere.

Never one to linger, Buzz departed, knowing each person had chosen what to receive from the gift. As he used to say, "What you give is what you get."

Index of Themes

Index of Settings

Reflection and Discussion Guide

Perhaps you are not finished with these stories, or these stories are not finished with you. Take some time to read through and answer the reflection questions. For a group, they can be used as discussion prompts. See if you can reveal what lives on from these stories.

Keep in mind the *Author's Take* is not the "correct" view of the story. These stories have a life of their own. Each person's experience with a particular story is as valid as the next person's view. Dig through the questions and see which ones bring life to you and your organization.

Deadline

About the Story

In a single word or phrase, what is this story about? What struck you about this story? Do you think it was Tricia's fault that she missed her deadline? Why? What else is this story about?

Bringing It Home

How is some aspect of this story a reflection of your life or career? What is a memory that you have that shows the effect deadlines have on your productivity? Can you describe a time when you suffered because of procrastination? What positive experience do you have with not procrastinating?

Author's Take

Procrastination. It plagues many of us. It feels so good to get things done ahead of schedule. We have heard this before, yet many of us avoid what we know we have to do, and in the meantime, we feel sick because of the stress it puts on us. It's been said that if we didn't procrastinate, we would be ahead of 90% of our competition. There is some truth to that. Yet many of us have trouble embracing it, or even reflecting on our own procrastinating behavior. On the other hand, most of us have noticed other people procrastinating. Perhaps we have advice for them that we could use ourselves.

Probation

About the Story

In a single word or phrase, what is this story about? What struck you about this story? Why do you think Marv was a good person to hire? What specifically did Marv do right? What else is this story about?

Bringing It Home

How is some aspect of this story a reflection of your life or career? What is a memory that demonstrates how persistence has paid off in your own career or personal life? What is one step you could take to help yourself to become more persistent?

Author's Take

Persistence is key. Those with it have a far better chance of succeeding than those without it. It is obviously important, but a quality many people lack. It is also a quality that we can cultivate in ourselves.

Ghosting

About the Story

In a single word or phrase, what is this story about? What struck you about this story? What do you think happened in Gene's life that led him to become the person he became? What else is this story about?

Bringing It Home

How is some aspect of this story a reflection of your life or career? What does integrity mean to you? What are the signs of a person of integrity? What is a positive memory of a time you did something of integrity?

Author's Take

Integrity matters. Not always, but if a person is cheating multiple times on his or her spouse, it is a good bet they will be cheating the company as well. If a person complains to you about everyone he or she knows, chances are that person complains about you as well. After all, you get what you see. A person of integrity is easy to spot over the long haul. Little things make up a breadcrumb trail to the big things.

Dead Serious

About the Story

In a single word or phrase, what is this story about? What struck you about this story? What are some of the factors you see in this story that led Sue to consider suicide? Could something like this actually happen? What else is the story about?

Bringing It Home

How is some aspect of this story a reflection of your life or career? What are successful ways that your organization helps people to reduce their stress levels? What works for you? Describe the last time you had a good laugh.

Author's Take

Self-care. We die without it. Stress and anxiety clearly hurt our health. They can kill us physically, mentally, emotionally, and socially. A good dose of humor can help us to relax and reduce our stress. Exercise, diet, workload, and healthy relationships are all hugely important. We need to be able to relax now and then. That helps us to be better at whatever we do. Those of us in the caring service professions need to have consistent ways to keep rejuvenated.

Down the Stairs

About the Story

In a single word or phrase, what is this story about? What struck you about this story? When did Melinda begin to fight back? What else is this story about?

Bringing It Home

How is some aspect of this story a reflection of your life or career? When have you had to take up a fight? In what situations have you exhibited the qualities of grit? Can you share a memory that demonstrates the difference between fighting back and revenge?

Author's Take

Self-preservation. We are hardwired for survival. All of us are called at times to fight back. It may not be in a physical sense. It could be emotional, social, or intellectual fights that we need to engage in, but we all need to defend ourselves. When we think that we don't have the strength to meet the challenge, the strength of grit comes into play. It is a survival instinct that rests in all of us.

The Founder

About the Story

In a single word or phrase, what is this story about? What struck you about this story? Why do think it was so hard for the founder to embrace change? Can you relate in some way to his mindset? What was he right about? What was he wrong about? What else is this story about?

Bringing It Home

How is some aspect of this story a reflection of your life or career? How do you embrace change? When have you been successful with a change initiative? What were the ingredients of that success? What changes would you like to make in the near future?

Author's Take

Change. Change is tricky business. Egos are involved. People don't like to be told what to do unless they understand and agree with why they must do it. Relationships change as duties and tasks evolve. Those changes put stress on interpersonal dynamics. That is huge. There is usually no training for it. It is no wonder many people dislike change. Plus, when we do something new, there is always a period of acquisition, that time of learning the new thing. We make mistakes when we do new things. Since we don't like to make mistakes, most of us have an impulse to avoid change. Yet, time marches on, and we have to keep up. Change is inevitable.

Mr. Baitenswitch

About the Story

Where did Brendan end up? In case you are unsure, he went to Mr. Baitenswitch's casket. In a single word or phrase, what is this story about? What struck you about this story? How did Brendan get drawn in to his anger? What else is this story about?

Bringing It Home

How is some aspect of this story a reflection of your life or career? What lessons have you learned from past experiences about getting angry? What is an example of how you learned one of those lessons? What is a memory of a time others got angry, but you did not? What tools does your organization have in place to help people with anger management? What more is needed?

Author's Take

Anger management. Control our temper. Bait and switch refers to the dishonest technique of tricking people into getting something they don't want. Angry people can bait us. If we take the bait, anger often takes us to a place we would not choose to go. When we lose control of our temper, we are the ones who end up in trouble. The good news is people can't actually telephone us from the grave, but most of us need special training in how to maintain our cool when things get heated. It is not easy to stay calm when people direct their anger at us or try to push our buttons.

Bottom Line

About the Story

In a single word or phrase, what is this story about? What struck you about this story? Is it realistic that people might have regrets even when they are in their chosen field and highly successful, and why? What else is this story about?

Bringing It Home

How is some aspect of this story a reflection of your life or career? What ways could cross-pollinating roles help an organization? What might that look like in your organization? What has your experience about dreams taught you? What other roles in your work would you like to try?

Author's Take

Cross-pollinate. Help people follow their interests. It is healthy for people to be involved in new things. Management does well to pay attention to dreams and cross-pollinate roles. Perhaps it is only for a day, or a week, or month, but wouldn't it be great if you got to try something else for a change, something you always wanted to do? OK, some of us don't want to try anything new, and some people wish they could do something but don't have the skill for it. That said, there are still ways to mix things up, follow emerging interests, and keep things fresh. When someone gets encouraged to follow a dream, there can be amazing results.

Working Dead

About the Story

In a single word or phrase, what is this story about? What struck you about this story? What do you think are some of the reasons Mercedes Jefferson ignored her gut feeling about Brian Tombwater? It's OK to go beyond what is written in the story. What else is this story about?

Bringing It Home

How is some aspect of this story a reflection of your life or career? What is a memory of a time you followed your gut instincts? Why do you believe or not believe in the value of gut instincts?

Author's Take

Instincts. Trust your instincts. Of course, first impressions aren't everything. A healthy person tries to keep an open mind about issues and people. There is always something new to learn. Yet, each of us has an amazing ability to get a sense of what is right, and occasionally, that happens very quickly. Sometimes we have to get out of our head. We need to trust our gut. It guides us on what to do, who to hire, and how to approach a situation. It works in tandem with our conscious thoughts. We often need more information to make an informed decision, but we should not discount our instincts.

Cold Hearted

About the Story

What is the narrator's office? The answer is the company refrigerator. In a single word or phrase, what is this story about? What struck you about this story? Which reactions to the teaching moments seemed realistic to you? Try to describe what a reaction might look like if the lesson had been learned? What else is this story about?

Bringing It Home

How is some aspect of this story a reflection of your life or career? What is a memory that demonstrates how you have been affected by struggles around the refrigerator or other common work areas? What might you do differently to not lose your cool? What is your vision of people effectively sharing space or equipment?

Author's Take

Perspective. Keep a healthy perspective always. Remember the little things are little. We all know that little things do matter, and personal space is important. If someone messes with your things in the refrigerator, it can be upsetting, but being upset doesn't help us to think straight. Each of us needs to find ways to take things in stride, to get along with others, to deal in healthy ways with small problems. Remember that it was a straw that broke the camel's back. Little problems need to be addressed as they surface, or they will lead to something worse.

Stone Faced

About the Story

In a single word or phrase, what is this story about? What struck you about this story? Why do you think Joseph felt the right to break the rules? Is that a common experience? What else is this story about?

Bringing It Home

How is some aspect of this story a reflection of your life or career? What are consequences that might happen in your organization when the rules are not followed? What rules often don't get followed? What rules seem unfair? How might they be adjusted?

Author's Take

Rules. They are for our own good and for the protection of our organizations. Every organization needs rules, but not every organization is good at explaining the reasons behind the rules. Some rules may seem arbitrary and others outdated. Many of us feel above the rules. When we go above and beyond our job description, it is easy to feel entitled to bend the rules to our needs and desires. We may feel that the company owes us at least that much. Healthy organizations are able to discuss and revise rules.

Into the Light

About the Story

In a single word or phrase, what is this story about? What struck you about this story? What did the manager do right? What would you have done if you were in the manager's position? What else is this story about?

Bringing It Home

How is some aspect of this story a reflection of your life or career? When have you addressed a problem successfully by following the instructions of another person? How do you try to share your own best practices?

Author's Take

Best practices. Learn from others. When we come across a problem that we haven't experienced, we can try to handle it all on our own, but it is wise to find out what others have done to rectify similar situations. We do well to learn from those who have come before us. We do well to listen to those closest to us. We do well to search for best practices.

Going Down

About the Story

In a single word or phrase, what is this story about? What struck you about this story? What do you notice about Bennett's behavior in this story? Do you agree that there is more than one way to die? What does that mean to you? What else is this story about?

Bringing It Home

How is some aspect of this story a reflection of your life or career? What are ways you attempt to keep your life in balance? What are some of your challenges? What specifically do you do to stay balanced?

Author's Take

Balance. Work-life and home-life balance is essential. We all need it. This is especially difficult when we care about something important and time consuming at work. Listening to the voice of wisdom is important but not easy. It can be difficult to tell what is the voice of wisdom. Sometimes we can't get work off our minds. Most of us have conflicting ideas in our head about what is most important. It is a helpful practice to regularly examine your own balance to assess how you are doing.

Dead Wrong

About the Story

In a single word or phrase, what is this story about? What struck you about this story? What part of the story seemed most realistic to you? What else is this story about?

Bringing It Home

How is some aspect of this story a reflection of your life or career? What is a project that you are working on that you are thankful you have a team working with you, and why? Describe a time you were part of a successful team. What did your team achieve, and how?

Author's Take

Teamwork. Five heads are better than one. Very few of us have the ability to do it all by ourselves or even the energy to try. So, we need teams if we are to strive for excellence. Sure, there is one part that we can do better than others, but we need a team to create a whole product or system. Of course, it is hard to get along with people. It takes work. It takes good communication. It takes shared vision.

Number One

About the Story

In a single word or phrase, what is this story about? What struck you about this story? What is one example from this story which shows Edmondson was not resilient? In what way was Edmondson metaphorically dead before he even died? What else is this story about?

Bringing It Home

How is some aspect of this story a reflection of your life or career? What does resilience mean to you? When are you at your best? How do you feel if you fall short of doing your best? Specifically, what is a healthy way to regroup and try again?

Author's Take

Resilience. The best salespeople have to be resilient. One definition of resilience is the ability to be able to recover quickly from difficulties. Setbacks can't ruin our day. Ambition is a great thing, but without resilience, it is next to impossible to achieve success. Knowing when to say enough is enough is a healthy quality. Remembering that we can't win them all can be a saving grace.

Bridge

About the Story

In a single word or phrase, what is this story about? What struck you about this story? What lessons can you draw from this story that you believe to be true? What else is this story about?

Bringing It Home

How is some aspect of this story a reflection of your life or career? What is one way you try to make sure that you listen to other people? When was a time when it felt like people truly listened to you?

Author's Take

Collaboration. It is often valuable to embrace joint decision-making. Organizations all over the world are trying to flatten their management system so that more voices of knowledge have a chance to be heard. Yet, it is not easy. Command and control seems a natural fit for many people in authority. Listening to others and sharing decision-making takes continual effort. The best leaders are strong listeners. This lesson goes far beyond an individual team or department. Effective companies keep open communication and joint decision-making as a company-wide practice.

Deadbeats

About the Story

In a single word or phrase, what is this story about? What struck you about this story? What might the narrator have done to try to fit in with the group? What else is this story about?

Bringing It Home

How is some aspect of this story a reflection of your life or career? In your work environment, what is an example of a way in which people are able to keep their independence and individuality?

Author's Take

Individuality. Be your own person. It is important to get along with others at work, yet we do not need to conform to ways that make us overly uncomfortable. Team members must use common sense to decide for themselves what to do to fit into a company culture and simultaneously be their own person.

Habits

About the Story

In a single word or phrase, what is this story about? What struck you about this story? Which character resonated with you the most, and why? What memory might Bob discover about himself? What else is this story about?

Bringing It Home

How is some aspect of this story a reflection of your life or career? Can you think of a habit that you have? Is it perhaps tied to a distant memory? What is a strong memory that has helped to shape whom you have become? Perhaps it was an affirmation that someone gave you long ago or a mistake you made that you vowed to never make again?

Author's Take

Self-awareness. It is good when we notice our behavioral patterns because they are there for all to see. There are many things we do without actively choosing to do them. They are the things that we seemingly always have done. They are the way we roll. Unfortunately, some of these behaviors are destructive, and it takes work to unveil them. Others are productive and are second nature to us. If we recognize them, we can get more of a good thing.

Dead of Winter

About the Story

In a single word or phrase, what is this story about? What struck you about this story? Why did Pablo come to the United States? What price did he pay for the trip? If you were Pablo, do you think you would have tried to escape the ICE agents, and why? What effect do you think this situation has on the ICE agents? What else is this story about?

Bringing It Home

How is some aspect of this story a reflection of your life or career? When have you seen an injustice at a place you worked? What is an example of how you have shown compassion toward others?

Author's Take

Compassion. Be compassionate. Try to reform injustice. Life is difficult, sometimes so much so that we are willing to break the rules. Think about that for yourself. If you were driving a dying family member to the hospital, chances are you would be willing to go through a red light. That is a tiny example of a much bigger issue. Desperate people do desperate things. Where undue hardship exists, we are better people when we work for reform, when we speak out for those less fortunate than ourselves. If lots of good people keep breaking the rules, it is an indication that compassionate change is needed. This isn't limited to immigration. There are opportunities for compassion every day.

Hot Seat

About the Story

In a single word or phrase, what is this story about? What struck you about this story? What are your best guesses of why Jack didn't respond to the people who contacted him? What else is this story about?

Bringing It Home

How is some aspect of this story a reflection of your life or career? Who are people you know who respond promptly and clearly? What's a story from your experience that demonstrates good communication? What are your best practices of good communication?

Author's Take

Communication. Take the time to communicate effectively. When we think about the people we like to work with, good communication is always a factor. We all know that, but practicing good communication can be a challenge. There are exceptions, but we are more likely to receive good communication when we offer it ourselves. When we ask someone a question, we expect an answer and vice versa. When we don't hear back, it can be upsetting, especially when it is a pattern. What goes around comes around.

Warmth

About the Story

In a single word or phrase, what is this story about? What struck you about this story? In what ways do you think Henry believed what he was saying to the children? What else is this story about?

Bringing It Home

How is some aspect of this story a reflection of your life or career? When are spoken words most powerful for you? What is a personal story that demonstrates how you, or someone else, spoke something out loud and changed a situation?

Author's Take

Words. Powerful words create our future. Words catch us. Sometimes we say things without thought or just to be funny. Sometimes we are even compelled to make things up that we hope will not happen. Voicing ideas often makes them stick in our minds. Speaking them out loud clarifies them. It is easy to find ourselves focusing on these things that we have said. We may not become shadow people, but sometimes we can become our own worst enemy. Of course, there is a very positive side to focusing on what we want and to speak it clearly. There is great benefit to choosing our words carefully.

Right Here

About the Story

In a single word or phrase, what is this story about? What struck you about this story? What would you have done if you were Shaneeka's boss? What else is this story about?

Bringing It Home

How is some aspect of this story a reflection of your life or career? Is it better to help one person completely or two people incompletely? When have you felt caught because you had more work to do than you had time available to do it? What was the outcome? How do you get through your busiest periods?

Author's Take

Coping. Do what we can. Sometimes there is no good way out of a situation. Occasionally, we have to choose between two unpleasant outcomes. Many people long to put people before numbers, but how do we do that? Many of us make lists of the things we want to accomplish in a day. It is a good habit, keeping track of what we are trying to do. Sometimes, however, we really just want to cross off everything on the list. Most of us have done something halfheartedly simply to get it off our list. There is a dilemma that arises from the fact that we can't do everything. Each of us needs to decide how we cope with that reality.

Stage Fright

About the Story

In a single word or phrase, what is this story about? What struck you about this story? Are the fears that John expressed common? Guess at how you think he did in his presentation. Why do you think that? What else is this story about?

Bringing It Home

How is some aspect of this story a reflection of your life or career? What helps you when you feel nervous? Share a time that you did well even though you were nervous beforehand.

Author's Take

Stage Fright. Don't be scared. It is OK to be nervous. It means that we have energy for what we are about to do. It means that we are going to have the chance to do something important for us. In this light, nervousness is good, yet it is still uncomfortable. We can ease this discomfort by imagining what success would look like. Professional athletes do this regularly and very specifically. Also, remember to keep things in perspective. Many times, an important presentation is not a matter of life or death. If things go wrong, we'll likely have a chance to try again another day. If it is a once in a lifetime opportunity, remember these three words. Prepare, prepare, prepare!

Undecided

About the Story

In a single word or phrase, what is this story about? What struck you about this story? What was the company doing? It was continuing to bill people who tried to cancel services. Why do you think Abe hadn't spoken up earlier? What else is this story about?

Bringing It Home

How is some aspect of this story a reflection of your life or career? Do you remember a time when you said one thing and then did another? Can you share an example of a time you were caught in something that was dishonest? How did you get involved, and what happened? How can an employee make a positive difference when questionable practices are being encouraged?

Author's Take

Honesty. Speak truth to power. It is true that not everything needs to be said. However, an environment where policies are put into place without permitting feedback is toxic. It kills morale, creativity, and loyalty. Strong leaders listen to the wisdom of dissenting voices. Unjust and dishonest practices must be exposed. When a toxic environment exists, all kinds of dysfunctional behaviors arise.

The Dust

About the Story

In a single word or phrase, what is this story about? What struck you about this story? What difference might it have made if the people in this story confided in one another? What else is this story about?

Bringing It Home

How is some aspect of this story a reflection of your life or career? What helps you to feel that you can trust others? Share a memory of a time you collaborated successfully with others. What part did trust play in that experience?

Author's Take

Trust others. It is important to have a circle of people we trust. When we hold on to important information, because we don't trust anyone else, we can make our own prison. We need to confide in others or find a new place where we can trust others. Collaboration and trust go hand and hand.

Gift Box

About the Story

In a single word or phrase, what is this story about? What struck you about this story? Which person reminded you of yourself? What else is this story about?

Bringing It Home

How is some aspect of this story a reflection of your life or career? What do you pay most attention to in your daily routine? Share a memory of a time that illustrates when you feel most satisfied.

Author's Take

Satisfaction. What we pay attention to is what we find. Where some people see nothing, others see countless possibilities. This is not a trivial observation. Gratitude stems from it. Satisfaction comes to us when we pay attention to what we have, rather than what we don't have.

About the Author

J. Thomas Sparough is a writer, performer, facilitator, and lover of ghost stories. He combines the skills of storytelling and experiential design in his colorful programs. His work is dedicated to unlocking wisdom in the world through engaging and unique experiences. He is especially interested in generative storytelling. His love of metaphor steers much of his writing.

He lives in Cincinnati, OH with his wife, Geralyn, who is also his organizational business partner. He is thankful that nearby are his children, grandchildren, mother-in-love, extended family, delightful neighbors, and spirits unseen.

Learn more about his work by visiting these websites:
SpacePainter.com
Creative-Retreat.net

Want to learn more about storytelling?

Consider joining the National Storytelling Network!

- Organizational storytelling
- Traditional storytelling
- Healing stories
- Ghost stories
- Personal narrative

Visit StoryNet.Org